Politics Transformed

Lula and the Workers' Party in Brazil

Sue Branford
and **Bernardo Kucinski**
with **Hilary Wainwright**

Latin America Bureau
LONDON

Politics Transformed: Lula and the Workers' Party in Brazil was
first published by
Latin America Bureau
1 Amwell Street
London EC1R 1UL
in 2003

Latin America Bureau is an independent research and publishing
organization. It works to broaden public understanding of issues of
human rights and social and economic justice in Latin America
and the Caribbean.

Editing: Jean McNeil
Cover design: Mariano Losi, Diseño Atlántico, Buenos Aires
Interior design and setting: Kate Kirkwood
Printed by J.W. Arrowsmith Ltd, Bristol

A CIP catalogue record for this book is available from the British Library.

ISBN 1 899365 61 3

Contents

Preface

The idea of writing this book arose on the wave of delight that swept over many of us in October when we realised that at last, on his fourth attempt, Lula was going to be elected President of Brazil. For several years there have been loud rumblings of discontent in Latin America at the social cost of the Washington Consensus, the name given to the free-market economic policies that, with the encouragement of the international financial community, almost all governments in the region have been pursuing with unswerving conviction for up to two decades. The fact that Brazil, the regional giant with a larger population than the rest of the countries in the continent put together, has elected its first working-class President on a platform of far-reaching social change is the most dramatic sign yet that the Latin American unrest could herald the construction of a real alternative to neo-liberalism.

I first met Lula on a wet afternoon in 1978. I went with other journalists to São Bernardo, on the outskirts of São Paulo, where workers at some of the huge multinational car assembly plants had organised one of the first big strikes to challenge the military government that had been in power for a decade and a half. We had heard that there was a lot of support for the strike but, even so, we were not prepared for what we saw – about 80,000 workers crammed into a football stadium because it was the only place big enough to hold them. The main speaker was Lula, president of the metalworkers' union in São Bernardo. I would like to say that I came back convinced that I had been listening to a future President of Brazil. That would not be true, but it had been clear that something important was happening. It had been pouring with rain, the sound system had not been working properly, and most people had not even been able to hear Lula distinctly, but there was something in the air – an excitement running through everyone in the crowd as they strained to listen to Lula – that convinced us that history was being made.

And history the striking workers certainly did make: first of all, by leading the movement that eventually sent the military back to the barracks, and then by setting up Brazil's first mass-based left-wing party, the Partido dos Trabalhadores (PT – the Workers' Party), which has now come to power in Brazil. No one knows yet what the PT will be able to achieve. Not the radical revolutionary overthrow of the state that so many on the left dreamed of in the 1960s and 1970s, for, as the Marxist historian Eric Hobsbawm has said, 'that is no longer possible'. But perhaps a social revolution to end the extraordinary inequalities in Brazil whereby, as the Brazilian novelist Antônio Callado put it, 'anyone in Brazil who every day has three meals, takes a shower and puts on a clean set of clothes belongs to the privileged elite'.

In this short book, we have brought together elements that will help people abroad to understand what is going on in Brazil. Based very loosely on a book on the PT that Bernardo Kucinski and I wrote earlier, we provide a brief history of that party, an account of Lula's earlier life, an analysis of the legacy that the PT is inheriting from eight years of the Cardoso government, and a look at its most exciting experiment in local government, in the city of Porto Alegre. Although all three contributors to this book share a common position of support for the PT, we differ in some aspects of our analysis.

We would like to express our gratitude to Alfredo Saad-Filho and to Harry Shutt for reading the manuscript at great speed and coming up with corrections and insightful suggestions and to Mike and Kate Kirkwood, Ralph Smith and Maria Prado for their valuable contributions to the editing of the book. All views expressed and any remaining errors are, of course, the sole responsibility of the authors. Above all, we would like to thank our publisher, Latin America Bureau, which had the audacity to seize the political moment and the flexibility to turn this book around at great speed.

Sue Branford
20 December 2002

Introduction

SUE BRANFORD

São Paulo's Avenida Paulista is a monument to money: the wide avenue is lined with the solid concrete and glass towers of giant banking corporations.* But on 27 October, election night, a sea of red flags lapped at the doors of the banks as thousands of supporters of the victorious PT (*Partido dos Trabalhadores*, or Workers' Party) waited for their hero, chanting campaign slogans. When he appeared on a giant screen making his acceptance speech men and women wept with joy – and disbelief. Was this really happening? After 13 years and three failed attempts at the presidency, was Luiz Inácio Lula da Silva really President of Brazil? Had the left wing finally come to power after 500 years of rule by the elite, the military, the landowners, the bankers?

About 3,000 kilometres to the north, in the poverty-stricken rural hamlet of Caetés in the interior of the state of Pernambuco, people poured out into the streets as soon as the election result was announced on television. Old people hugged each other. Young people danced around the *trio elétrico* (a procession float), decked out in the Workers' Party's distinctive red flags, as it made its way through the streets blaring carnival music. Fireworks went off. Here in the so-called 'Republic of the Silvas' nearly everyone carries the surname and is – or claims to be – a relative of the new President. 'We never thought it would happen', said a cousin, 53-year-old José Ricardo Silva. 'We just dreamed it would, like we dream each year of rain.'

1

Lula was born in Caetés in 1945, on 6 October (also the date of the first round of the 2002 election) according to his birth certificate or on 27 October (the date of the second round of the election) according to his mother, Eurídice Ferreira de Mello, who died 20 years ago. When Lula was seven years old, his mother got into a *pau-de-arara* (open lorry) with her eight children and made the 13-day journey down to São Paulo to find work. Lula made the return journey to Caetés in 2002. 'Almost nothing's changed', he said. 'The same backwardness, the same corrupt politics that have always plagued this region.'

In the days following the election Lula was mobbed wherever he went. Papers ran stories about 'Saint Lula', and people began to idolise the man who, like millions of other Brazilians, began life in abject poverty, but was now President-elect of the world's fourth-largest democracy and tenth-largest economy. Yet Lula is constantly disassociating himself from Brazil's long tradition of powerful messianic leaders: the Workers' Party he helped found in the early 1980s deliberately set out to limit the power of its leaders and to make them accountable to the mass of party members, thought to number about 600,000. The PT has not found all the answers, for there is still an uneasy tension between the party itself and its municipal and state administrations, which necessarily have to rule for the whole population, but it has gone much further than almost any other political party in the world towards making itself truly democratic.

Moreover, the party has established a new kind of participatory, grassroots democracy in cities and states under its control. The mechanism it has created is the so-called 'participatory budget' (*orçamento participativo*), which allows ordinary people, whether members of the PT or not, to have a say in how government revenue is spent. Many *petistas* (PT members) are keen to extend this practice to a federal level, though they know this will be fraught with difficulties. One of Brazil's oldest and most influential left-wing economists, Celso Furtado, has been saying for years that if Brazil is really to construct a radically new form of participatory democracy then the government must open up decision-making: 'The point of departure for any new alternative project for the nation must necessarily involve an increase in participation and in popular power in the country's decision-making centres.'[1] Although Furtado is calling for something more radical than the participatory budget, the PT is the only political party to have made any move in this direction.

Furtado is hoping that the PT will be taking up a project that he tried in 1962. In the very different circumstances of that time, as planning minister in the government of President João Goulart, he was part of the project to redistribute land, income, and wealth and to democratise the educational and political systems. Furtado's initiative came to an abrupt end with the military coup in 1964, but his reformist ideas never completely disappeared. They survived in embryonic form, first in the resistance movement against the military government and then in the 'new unionism' that paved the way for the creation of the Workers' Party. They were evident in the text of the progressive 1988 Constitution, particularly in the chapters on the civil, social, political and economic rights of Brazilian citizens. Many *petistas* will be hoping that the time has finally arrived for Brazil to implement a project for a more democratic and inclusive society in which the state, reviled during the last decade of free-market reforms, will regain a key role.

The new PT government is widely seen as the most exciting political development in Latin America since the election of the Marxist Salvador Allende in Chile in 1970; it will be watched closely throughout the world. It has come at a time when the region is challenging more than two decades of dutiful and painful subservience to the IMF's neo-liberal reforms. In Venezuela Hugo Chávez – who, unlike Lula, does indeed project himself as the 'saviour of the poor' – was somewhat unexpectedly elected to power in December 1998 because of widespread disillusion with old, corrupt political parties.

However, without the support of a solid and self-sustaining political party like the PT, and despite his remarkable survival skills, Chávez seems doomed to fail in his crusade to redistribute income and break the power of the moneyed elites. In Argentina, the population is searching for a new way forward after the spectacular collapse of the neo-liberal project in December 2001. Through the *piquetes* and the *asambleas populares*, grassroots groups have created inspiring forms of local participatory democracy, but these new forms of organisation are still far from developing a national alternative to the discredited and corrupt traditional political parties. In Bolivia, Evo Morales, an Aymara indigenous leader running on a strongly anti-neoliberal programme, came close to winning the presidential elections in August 2002. And in Ecuador a coalition of indigenous groups and left-wing movements won the presidential elections on 20 October 2002 in a remarkable setback for the traditional political parties, which had expected to win. The PT's victory in Brazil's presidential election has been the biggest gain for the left so far. If the party can successfully break out of the constraints it has inherited from the Cardoso government, then Brazil could lead a continent-wide search for a real alternative to neo-liberalism.

This would be a radical departure for Brazil. Although it is by far the largest country in Latin America and has borders with ten countries, Brazil has never assumed the leadership role commensurate with its geographical size and economic might. When the former left-wing sociologist Fernando Henrique Cardoso was elected President in 1994, he promised to develop an independent foreign policy and to become a spokesman for the region. But this never happened. Despite a strong personal attachment to French culture, Cardoso aligned Brazil firmly with the United States, apparently believing that the country would benefit from strengthening its ties with the world's superpower and endorsing free market economics. Apart from relatively minor squabbles over generic drugs, aeroplanes and orange juice, relations with Washington were harmonious.

Will the PT change this? Will it stand up to the United States at a time when Washington is working to strengthen its hegemony over the region in order to impose the Free Trade Area of the Americas (FTAA), the largest free trade area in the world? The North American Free Trade Area (NAFTA) has served US interests well in turning Mexico into a source of cheap labour for multinationals and a market for US industrial and agricultural products. Although the urgency with which the US is pursuing the FTAA goal has faltered as other more urgent issues have claimed its attention at home and abroad, its desire to incorporate, one by one, the other Latin American nations into a giant expansion of NAFTA is the driving force in US policy towards Latin America. Can Lula be the spearhead for a regional movement of resistance? Does the PT even want to take on this role?

Over the last two or three years the PT has reinvented itself as a moderate left-wing party. In 1998, shortly after his third defeat in the presidential race, Lula made it clear to the PT national leadership that he would agree to run a fourth time only if he were given a free hand to form alliances across the political board and was provided with the resources to run a slick, professional electoral campaign. The new strategy, which Lula devised with the PT's chairman, José Dirceu (who spent the late 1960s being an urban guerrilla and who was released from jail as a consequence of the spectacular kidnapping of the US ambassador in Rio), was endorsed by the leadership and then rigorously enforced. The PT ran an all-inclusive presidential campaign in which, with the support of some sugary and politically dubious TV commercials built around the slogan 'Lula, Peace and Love', it sought to win over those sectors of society that traditionally had been hostile to it, particularly the business community. It selected Senator José Alencar from the small right-of-centre Liberal Party as Lula's running-mate. Alencar, who owns Brazil's largest textile company, Coteminas, and has a personal fortune of about US$500 million, is progressive to the extent that he pays his workers a decent wage – at least by Brazilian standards – and allows them to form independent unions, but he is still clearly part of the business establishment. He is also a nationalist.

Many of the PT's oldest supporters, above all left-wing intellectuals, were horrified at what they perceived as a deeply compromised and cosmetic makeover, particularly because the Liberal Party is closely linked to the socially conservative evangelical Universal Church of the Kingdom of God. 'It's no secret that, at first, I was against the alliance with the Liberal Party', said Antônio Cândido, a leading intellectual and one of the founders of the Workers' Party, in an interview in mid-2002.[2]

> Lula even mentioned the fact that both I and Marilena Chauí [a lecturer in philosophy at the University of São Paulo and Culture Secretary in the first PT administration in São Paulo] were opposed, in an interview with the *Folha de S. Paulo*. Lula said that, while we were intellectuals, he was a politician and had to follow another logic. But then, after the decision, I accepted it. I think it's so important for Brazil that Lula wins this election that I'll accept any alliance that he deems necessary. And I'm still confident that, once elected, he and the party will change this country.

Lula's strategy worked. Old opponents were won over. Eugênio Staub, chief executive of a leading hi-fi company, Gradiente, decided to back Lula publicly, even though he is a close friend of the other main candidate, José Serra, and earlier had said that he would vote for him. He took his decision after holding several secret meetings with Lula. 'Serra is a competent and very intelligent man, but the international moment is extremely critical for Brazil', he explained. 'We need someone in the presidency who is 100 per cent a politician. And Lula is a real statesman. He is the only person who can unite labour, business and other broad social sectors. And that's what Brazil needs today.'[3] Millions took the same decision as Staub, and voted for a man they had rejected in the past. Lula won the second round of the elections with a large majority. Afterwards he commented that he had won just as he had always dreamed of winning: in a clean contest without personal abuse or dirty tricks.

Lula's victory was greeted with euphoria at home and a largely positive reception abroad. 'I think Lula's triumph is a key moment in Brazil's history, like the abolition of slavery or the proclamation of the Republic', commented Francisco de Oliveira, a leading sociologist. 'It may be the point at which we move on from a passive history, in which the country is led by the dominant blocs, to an active history in which the dominated classes have a big impact on state policies.' 'The result of the election is important, not just for Brazil, but for the rest of the world', said Boaventura de Sousa Santos, economics professor at the University of Coimbra in Portugal. 'With the coming to power of the Workers' Party, Brazil is finally completing the long transition from the 21 years of military rule.' And the British historian Eric Hobsbawm commented: 'The PT's victory is one of the few events at the beginning of the twenty-first century that gives us hope for the rest of the century. The PT is a new force in the history of Brazil.'[4]

The flurry of new projects it has already outlined announce the PT government's intention to carry out a far-reaching social revolution and to incorporate within the market and within society the millions of excluded Brazilians. At the same time, it is prepared to move slowly, working within the Constitution and accepting financial responsibility for the mistakes and even the corrupt practices of its predecessors. As Lula has made clear, his government will continue with the praxis of highly responsible and fiscally prudent government that the PT has established in its municipal and state administrations: 'We'll begin by doing what's necessary, then what's possible, and one day we'll wake up and find we're doing the impossible.' Eric Hobsbawm, a lifelong Marxist, suggests, not without a touch of regret, that this is perhaps the only way of achieving revolutionary change today: 'It hasn't happened as we hoped. The revolution that we wanted – and is still necessary in so many countries – hasn't happened and now it won't happen in Latin America.'[5]

Yet however conciliatory the approach that the government adopts, there will be defining moments. As a result of the Cardoso government's uncritical and wholesale adherence to the free-market economic model, the country is perilously vulnerable to foreign speculators. While medium-term prospects for economic recovery are fairly good, Brazil is heavily dependent in the short term on the good will of the International Monetary Fund (IMF) and foreign banks, if it is to avoid default. By delaying until early 2003 the disbursement of the bulk of the US$30-billion credit line announced in August 2002, the IMF has attempted to fence in the PT government. In practice it has told the Lula government that either it toes the line and runs a primary fiscal surplus (that is, before interest payments) equivalent to at least 3.75 per cent of GDP, or it will be denied the funds it needs to pay its foreign creditors. At the time this book went to press, the Lula government appeared to have accepted the IMF's demand, but this, too, creates a dangerous precedent, in that it encourages the international financial community in its belief that it can hold Brazil to ransom. The PT government will soon be faced by a stark alternative: either it will have to confront the rage of foreign investors and impose capital controls, or it will have to surrender ultimate responsibility for policy making to foreign creditors.

Lula himself is well aware of the conflicting pressures on his government. He once asked Brazil's social movements to carry on with their mobilisations (from what he called a 'fraternal' standpoint). Brazil's powerful Landless Movement (*Movimento dos Trabalhadores Rurais Sem Terra*, or MST), one of the largest social movements in the world, does not need to be asked.

While it was delighted by Lula's victory, the MST has learnt from its long history of direct action that it gets what it wants only through constant mobilisation. João Pedro Stédile, the most prominent of the MST leaders, has called for a 'mass movement in favour of change' that will act as a counterweight to the pressure from the foreign creditors. 'If Lula is involved in the movement, then we will support him', he said. 'If on the contrary he tries to deceive the people and asks for our unending patience, then he will end up like de la Rúa [the deposed Argentine president].'[6]

Lula will need enormous political skill to pilot the new government through a rough sea of conflicting and entrenched agendas. While many commentators have questioned Lula's ability, pointing to his lack of administrative experience and his low level of education (which caused Lula on one famous occasion to joke, not without a touch of sarcasm, that he and George W. Bush must be 'the most ignorant presidents on the earth'), others are fervent in their support. One of his admirers, Antônio Cândido, has little time for Lula's detractors. 'People are very stupid when they criticise Lula for being uneducated', he said.

Lula is very intelligent, and his intelligence makes up for his lack of formal education. Lula has an extraordinary capacity for absorbing information and re-elaborating it in a way that is useful to him. I've known Lula for more than 20 years and I've seen him do it on numerous occasions. Brazil has tried having an intellectual as President and it didn't work. Intellectuals aren't made for power. To be in power you need to be a leader. And Lula is an extraordinary leader. Like all great leaders, he embodies the profound aspirations of the Brazilian people. The Brazilian people speak through him. He represents them. At first, he did it unconsciously and now he does it consciously. His leadership can unleash a process of revolutionary change in the country.

Notes

* This chapter incorporates, with her consent, part of an article by Jan Rocha for the North American Congress on Latin America (NACLA).

1 Celso Furtado, *Brasil, a Construcção Interrompida*, 1992.

2 Interview conducted by the PT and published on its website, *Lula Presidente*.

3 In an interview with the Argentine newspaper, *Clarin*, 29 September 2002.

4 *Folha de S. Paulo*, 13 November 2002.

5 Ibid.

6 See Sue Branford and Jan Rocha, *Cutting the Wire: the Story of Brazil's Landless Movement*, Latin America Bureau, London, 2002.

1
The Rise of the Workers' Party

BERNARDO KUCINSKI

While socialism declined in the West during the final decades of the twentieth century, the Brazilian left created three new forms of popular organisation that took the left by surprise in other countries. These were: the Workers' Party (PT), a new strong trade union confederation called *Central Única dos Trabalhadores* (CUT), and the nation-wide Landless Workers' Movement or *Movimento dos Trabalhadores Rurais Sem Terra* (MST). The Workers' Party lay at the heart of these unprecedentedly large organisations, which not only shared similar dreams of social transformation but often the same members and leaders. After growing slowly at first, the PT suddenly won two consecutive landslide victories at the beginning of the twenty-first century, first electing an impressive number of mayors in Brazil's major cities in 2000, and then, in 2002, first getting more members into Congress and into the state government assemblies than any other party, and then having its main leader and one of its founder members – the former metalworker Luíz Inácio Lula da Silva, nicknamed 'Lula' – elected President of Brazil by a massive majority.

Lula's election had above all an emblematic dimension: it was the first time in Brazil's history – and in the history of Latin America since the Mexican revolution – that the son of a dis-possessed peasant had reached the pinnacle of political power. The implications of his victory are far-reaching both within Brazil and without, as can be gauged by the size of the Brazilian economy (the tenth-largest in the world), the continental dimension of the country, and its strategic position in Latin America.

The prospect of a left-wing government in power in Brazil sent shivers down the spine of global finance. But it also raised great expectations among Brazil's voters, demoralised by two decades of neo-liberal policies that had destroyed much of Brazil's social fabric and taken unemployment and violence to unprecedented levels. Lula was not elected with a mandate to put an end to capitalism, far less to do so by revolutionary means, but he was clearly elected – and with a massive majority, for that matter – with a mandate to completely change priorities in Brazil. The new concerns are to care for ordinary people, in particular the poor; to combat drug-trafficking; to restore national dignity; and to implement public policies for housing, health, public transport and education, sectors that during the neo-liberal era were either altogether neglected or subordinated to the priority of servicing the foreign and domestic debt and reducing the fiscal deficit.

The contradictions that emerged from neo-liberalism during the last years of the Cardoso government were so intense that Lula won with the support of a substantial part of the middle classes, and even with a degree of support from the ruling elite. In fact, one of the many ironies of Lula's rise to power is that while concepts such as 'social pact' were anathema at the birth of the Workers' Party in 1980, Lula explicitly asked for the support of the ruling elite during his campaign and, immediately after his victory, he proposed the formation of such a pact between workers and employers, so that the country's problems can be resolved on a consensual basis. Even so, one of the questions his experiment in power will have to answer is the extent to which the ruling elite and the upper classes are prepared for compromise and will submit to the leadership of the Workers' Party.

And will the United States' imperium, now in an era of expansion and reaffirmation of its rule worldwide, accept a left-wing government in power in Brazil, as part of a broader rejection of free-market economics in Latin America? Not only the PT, but other left and centre-left parties expanded their influence in the 2002 elections. Lula should be able to negotiate majority support in both houses of Congress; the total number of seats held by the left in the federal Chamber of Deputies went up by 40 per cent, from 112 to 161. Oligarchical and corrupt politicians were ousted in several parts of the country. There was a political revival and renewal of the left, which the conservative camp has called the 'red windfall'. Combined with Lula's election with an impressive 57.2 million votes (over 61 per cent of the votes cast), this development marks an important change in the balance of power in Brazil.

This process naturally attracted the attention of the world, particularly in Latin America, where most countries are undergoing one crisis or another, all of them very serious. The victory of Lula and the PT is being seen by the rest of the world, right and left alike, as perhaps the dawn of a new era, certainly the start of a new experiment in democracy. For Latin America, Lula's rise to power could pave the way for the development of alternative policies opposed to the monetarist recipes that have been imposed on the sub-continent by successive IMF missions since the start of the 1982 foreign debt crisis, and which have led to two decades of economic stagnation and social misery.

Argentinians, Peruvians, Bolivians, Venezuelans, Ecuadoreans and Cubans are seeing Lula's rise to power and his administration as a new experiment in radical democracy, an experiment that could give Latin America's formal democracies the social content they have so far lacked. For the left, Lula's victory paves the way for a new debate on the relationship between socialism and democracy, based on a real experiment in a big country. Lula and the PT's theoretical thinkers believe that the left has not yet developed a more comprehensive ideological answer to neo-liberal hegemony. They have won an election but they have not won power, in the sense of exerting hegemony. This hegemony still has to be built, by changing, first of all, the nature of the state apparatus, which is quite large and has been deployed since its creation by the Portuguese 500 years ago as an instrument of class domination. Particularly worrying for the PT is the domination by the right of Brazil's judiciary, which may prove more of a headache for the PT than Congress. The PT has only a four-year mandate to build a new hegemony and change that, while also changing the culture of Brazil's state bureaucracy.

Whatever the results of this experiment, Lula's 2002 election campaign will enter the history of democracy as a landmark and a case study of a people that decided to take destiny into its own hands. One of the reasons why Lula was defeated in three previous campaigns was that his opponents claimed he was not fit to rule as he lacked formal education. The majority of ordinary Brazilians, who also lack a comprehensive formal education and have known at least once or twice in their lives what it is like to go hungry or not to have the money to buy medicine, decided in 2002 not to submit to this argument, but to identify with Lula. This process raised the self-esteem of Brazilian voters and changed their mentality, defeating the established assumption that only the elite is entitled to rule. Lula was elected as the hero of a psychologically liberated Brazil. This has given him an extraordinary momentum and enviable political capital with which to start his government.

The coming-of-age of the PT

The PT emerged in the wake of a series of major strikes in the late 1970s that mortally wounded the military dictatorship (it was then given the *coup de grâce* by the huge nationwide mobilisations in 1983 and 1984 for the right to elect the country's President on a direct vote). The protagonists of the country's belated process of industrialisation, the metalworkers, helped create and then led a party that also arrived late on the scene. The metalworkers' strikes occurred at a time when the military dictatorship was faltering. In 1975 Vladimir Herzog, a well-known television news editor, had been arrested and killed under torture at the notorious CODI–DOI headquarters of the security forces. Just a few months later, in January 1976, an industrial worker, Manoel Fiel Filho, died in similar circumstances. In 1977 students took to the streets. By then intellectuals were calling for an amnesty for political offences and for the restoration of democracy. New trade union leaders, meanwhile, had emerged from under the protective cloak of the 'liberation theology' wing of the Catholic Church and were rejecting the old trade-union structures that had been taken over by the employers. All these forces contributed to the creation of the PT.

When it was founded, the PT attracted traditionally incompatible groups – Trotskyist and Leninist groups, Marxists and Catholics from the liberation wing of the Catholic Church, nearly illiterate workers and renowned intellectuals. In just a few years this alliance of opposites managed to become the first mass party in Brazil with predominantly socialist ideas, and the only mainstream political party with activists and a life outside electoral periods. In fact, the PT had a level of activism as great as that of the old communist parties, which had operated clandestinely during most of their existence in Brazil and which, for this and other reasons, had developed a conspiratorial political culture. In contrast, from the very beginning the Workers' Party held the view that politics must be exercised in the open, in the public sphere, and within a democratic framework.

For many years the PT remained a minor party. This was partly because the core of the working class that gave birth to the party – the car industry workers – lost its vitality during the following decade. Even so, after a period of slow growth in electoral support in the years immediately following its foundation in 1980, the PT grew rapidly. In the municipal elections in November 1988, the last to be held under the old

Constitution, the PT unexpectedly elected 36 mayors, including Luiza Erundina in São Paulo. The swing towards the PT may have been helped by public revulsion at the deaths of three workers after the army was sent in to break up a strike at the Volta Redonda steel mill. And then, in 1989, Lula came within an inch of winning the presidency at his first attempt. Instead, after a very dirty political campaign, Fernando Collor de Mello, who came from a traditional ruling family from the north-east (and was later to be forced out of office by massive mobilisations against his corruption), pipped him at the post. By the early 1990s the PT was the strongest party on the Brazilian left, although it was still a minority voice in the country's overall political spectrum. By then the PT had local party committees in 3,600 towns and around 600,000 members, two-thirds of whom were regular participants in the party's activities, a grass-roots militancy not found in other parties in Brazil. As early as 1988, the PT received 12.8 per cent of the vote – almost as much as each of the three major centre and right-wing parties – in the elections for the Federal Chamber of Deputies, which elects its members by a system of proportional representation. It also elected seven senators and 60 deputies in the Federal Congress, making it the fourth-largest party. It became a pole of attraction for Brazil's parliamentary opposition and consolidated its hegemony on the left.

But the final years of the decade were not easy ones for the PT. With a significant increase in unemployment, the CUT, which had 20 million affiliates, lost some of its influence to the 'business unionism' promoted by populist unions. The PT was also unable to capture the support of the middle classes, who were attracted by neo-liberal ideas, and lost some ideological and organisational ground to Marxist parties – the PCdoB (Communist Party of Brazil) and the PSTU (*Partido Socialista dos Trabalhadores Unificado*) – in the student movement. Later the PSTU joined the PT, but the PCdoB remained the dominant force among left-wing students. At the end of the 1990s other groups of workers who had participated in the creation of the PT, such as bank clerks, were also greatly weakened by the technological revolution, industrial decline and unemployment. The PT, however, did not disappear. On the contrary, it continued slowly to grow, gaining support from new sectors of society, such as the impoverished lower middle class and other dissatisfied groups.

Then, in the municipal elections in 2000, the first landslide on a national scale took place, partly in response to growing disillusion with Fernando Henrique Cardoso: party candidates received about 12 million votes, about one fifth of the total, and gained control of many large cities, including some state capitals, one of which was São Paulo, the world's third-largest metropolis. The breakthrough was largely due to the public perception of the PT as the only political force that was different. It was left-wing, which the public viewed with greater receptivity as a result of growing disillusion with Cardoso's free-market reforms, particularly after the spectacular collapse of the currency, the *real*, in late 1999. And it was the only party that included ethics as part of its political programme (and put that programme into practice in the municipalities where it was in power). By then, the press had fully exposed the corruption inherent in the way the neo-liberal model was being implemented. By capitalising on the public's disgust with corruption and with neo-liberalism in general, the PT received an avalanche of votes. These results changed the party's ranking in Brazilian politics and helped it to emerge in pole position in the 2002 presidential election.

Lula was the natural candidate. He had already run as the main left-wing candidate in the three presidential elections held after the end of the dictatorship – in 1989, 1994 and 1998. In these elections Lula's candidacy had presented a dramatic alternative to existing power structures, in the context of the extreme poverty suffered by about a third of the Brazilian population. He had therefore been considered unacceptable by the elites, who resorted to intensive manipulation of the media to prevent him winning. Even so, he had almost won in the first election, in 1989, gaining 47 per cent of the valid votes in the second round. In each successive election he gained more votes in the first round – 16 per cent in 1989, 22 per cent in 1994 and 26 per cent in 1998. He was the party's main vote-catcher and this was why he ran in all the elections, even when his chance of winning was very slight. Besides being a national leader, Lula has always been a diligent and industrious party cadre.

The 2002 election was different: with hindsight, Lula's victory seemed pre-ordained (although it did not always feel like that to his supporters at the time). By then, neo-liberalism was clearly suffering a crisis of legitimacy. The metaphor for its fiasco was the energy shortage in 2001, which followed the hasty privatisation of a substantial part of Brazil's formidable hydro-electric infrastructure. The shortage affected deeply both the day-to-day life of ordinary Brazilians and economic activity in general. People began to question the neo-liberal model, which had failed to keep many of its promises and had been damaged by the revelations of corruption that accompanied its imple-mentation. Throughout Latin America, the neo-liberal model was in collapse. This enabled the PT, helped by its 'clean' record in local government and its efforts to stamp out political patron-age, to gain the confidence of broad sectors of the middle classes. The PT was also known – and chastised for it by the media – as the most persistent critic of neo-liberal policies. It was only natural for the PT to profit from the neo-liberal fiasco in Brazil.

But the scale of the victory went beyond the most optimistic forecasts. Although the PT elected only three state governors in 2002, and lost the emblematic governorship of Rio Grande do Sul, this election marked the rise of the Workers' Party to the rank of Brazil's foremost political party, with more members of Congress (91) and more seats in State Assemblies (147) than any other party; it also became the only party with seats in all

26 state assemblies and the Federal District (Brasília). As had happened on several previous occasions, the PT failed to win many key state governorships by just a small fraction of votes – São Paulo, Federal District, and even Rio Grande do Sul. Altogether, PT candidates for state governorships received 21.13 million votes in 2002, compared with 9.56 million votes in 1998 and only 6.7 million votes in 1994. The PT candidates were among the top three in 21 of Brazil's 26 states, including all the most populous states such as São Paulo, Minas Gerais, Rio de Janeiro and Bahia. The swing to the PT in Bahia and some other states traditionally ruled by the landed oligarchy was massive, indicating a marked decline in the system of power based on clientelism and corruption.

The PT as an open political system

The Workers' Party defies definition. It was created by union leaders, rather as European social democracy was created at the beginning of the twentieth century, but it does not fit any model, not even that of the British Labour Party with which it has some similarities. Margaret Keck, author of the seminal study of the Workers' Party, called her work 'the study of an anomaly'.[1] In contrast with the Labour Party, the PT never had formal links with the trade unions, nor is it funded by them. It is supported by many Catholic activists, but defends equal rights for homosexuals and is willing to consider the legalisation of abortion. It is a mass party, operating openly, yet it is structured like a Leninist party, with a central committee and strict rules about adherence to party decisions (although, in practice, these rules are often broken). At the same time, and even more paradoxically, it allows the existence of organised tendencies within the party. Its supporters are active members of the many social movements in Brazil and are leaders of many of them, but the movements are not affiliated to the party and often clash with elected PT local authorities. Is the PT some kind of outdated

Marxist phenomenon or the precursor of a new kind of political organisation?

The PT could be tentatively described as an 'open' party, just as there are 'open' works of art to which anyone can contribute. It is, indeed, a political work of art. When the party was created, it welcomed everybody who wished to join. This process is still a central feature of the PT and explains the paradoxical 'PT democracy', in which opposites coexist, and only rarely do sectarian disputes prevail over the aims that unify the party. Initially, various left-wing groups joined the PT with the clear aim of using it for their own purposes, each one hoping to achieve hegemony over the new party. For example, one of the main groups, *Democracia Socialista*, which had Trotskyist roots, saw the PT as a transitional organisation. Its members joined the PT but have maintained their own party structure and their links with the Fourth International ever since.[2]

None of these groups managed to replace or take control of the PT, despite intense and sometimes cannibalistic internal struggle. The sectarian culture was slowly overcome by the way this mass party operated. However, the 'attraction of opposites', as Margaret Keck called it – the coexistence of different tendencies and schools of thought within the same party, each one bowing to the decisions of the majority – is still a hallmark of the PT.

A new contradiction may affect the party following the 2002 election. As it got a massive majority of the votes and elected new representatives all over the country, it reached an electoral density that does not fit into a party structured around cadres and narrow political groups. This contradiction will appear, for instance, when the party holds its primary elections: there is no longer any logic to limiting participation in the primaries to cadres only, as established by statute.

PT culture: ethics and radicalism

To understand this 'open' party, we need to know what it is that keeps the *petistas* together, besides a vague adherence to socialism. It is not a particular definition of socialism, far less a specific recipe on how to achieve it, but an ethos, an attitude towards society and political involvement that combines radicalism, self-denial and moral outrage. This is the common denominator of all *petistas*, be they intellectuals, workers, Catholics, agnostic activists, members of the MST or organisers of women's rights groups. An activist within a particular movement or community who is a radical and does not act out of self-interest will probably be a *petista*. This attitude is both a means of self-identification and an act of defiance against the dominant traits in Brazil's political culture: conciliation, tolerance and mutual self-interest.

The *petista* ethos, associated with the party since its creation, has become the party's indelible trademark. It explains many of the PT's characteristics: its inability to act opportunistically, which was particularly evident in the early stage of its development; its lack of interest in short-term political gains; and its resistance to political horse-trading. In the eyes of voters, *petismo* stands for morality in politics. Many PT adversaries, however, are irritated by what they see as an arrogant and self-righteous attitude of moral superiority.

In case vague adherence to these values was not enough to ensure appropriate behaviour by party members, the first party congress in 1981 approved a code of party ethics, making these values obligatory:

> The PT is a different kind of party, and we have a duty to develop a new and different set of party ethics, and express it clearly in our statutes. The new party political ethics must be based on four principles: first, the individual attitude of its activists; second, the relationships between activists; third, the concept of party loyalty; and fourth, the relations of the party and its activists with the out-

side world. By the first principle, we mean individual political integrity, that, for example, does not allow anyone holding office to advance his or her own personal position through political patronage, even though this may be common practice in the bourgeois system. Second, it is essential that activists act in a fraternal way to each other. Third, the concept of party loyalty in the PT has to show clearly that the party is more than the simple sum of its parts. Fourth, what is accepted as normal by other politicians does not mean that the PT should follow suit.[3]

This ethical code meant that in the beginning the party lost political opportunities because of its reluctance, often on moral grounds, to make agreements and alliances. However, as the PT began to elect mayors and state governments, it became more institutionalised and dropped much of this purism. Its grassroots activism lost some of its initial altruism as party cadres were given jobs in local authorities. It was also affected by a few isolated cases of corruption, nepotism and careerism. Although these cases, dominant in Brazilian political culture, were rare in the PT, they provoked strong internal reactions, in particular among intellectuals.

The *petista* ethos is traced back by social scientists to the base Christian communities (CEBs) and other mass-based movements that mushroomed in Brazil in the 1970s. There were hundreds of small organisations, mostly formed by migrants who came to the big cities in the south from the impoverished north-east. At its height the 80,000 CEBs alone had an estimated membership of two million.[4] The migrants had to construct their lives in the cities in very difficult conditions. With little help from the authorities, they had to build themselves a shack, get a job and sort out the other problems of everyday life.

These were the elements that in the past had underpinned populism in Brazil and elsewhere in Latin America. Though not really committed to migrant families, the typical populist leader built up his prestige and electoral strength by providing them with public services. But Brazil in the 1970s was being ruled by the military, which harshly repressed all kinds of political activity, including populism. Nor could the newcomers get help from the clandestine left-wing parties, which were nearly destroyed. Into this vacuum stepped the progressive wing of the Catholic Church, encouraged by the 'preferential option for the poor' made by Latin American bishops at the Medellín Conference in 1968. Some priests and lay leaders of the liberation theology wing of the church are also PT activists.[5]

With the Church's backing, the migrants could meet and work out how to satisfy their basic needs – how to bring water into their community, how to get the council to create a new bus route to take them to work, how to run self-help schemes for building more permanent homes. In this way, they developed the qualities of self-reliance and solidarity and learned how to take control of their own lives, building their own identity through the process of organising themselves. In so doing, they began to believe that they could challenge the system that was making their lives so difficult. In the early 1970s, as working conditions in the big factories temporarily worsened, the influence of these activists spread to the trade unions, originating a 'new unionism'. Driven by the same values, new unionism eventually led to the formation of a new political party, the PT.

The new unionism rejected the official trade union policy by which the government co-opted or even bribed trade union officials, known as *pelegos*,[6] to end labour conflicts. In 1974, during a metalworkers' congress in São Bernardo, the new unionism launched its first public manifesto, rejecting *pelego* unionism. The unions controlled by the Communist Party were partly involved in *pelego* unionism, as they had accepted the rules of the game, operating by means of opportunistic zigzags. In sharp contrast, new unionism demanded full union freedom and the right to negotiate collective work contracts. It was also critical of the trade union tax, equivalent to one day's wages per year, which was collected by the labour ministry from all employees and distributed to different unions. The tax allowed unions to survive whether or not they had support from the workforce, and encouraged corruption and the manipulation of the unions by government. The leaders of the new unionism were more concerned with the welfare of workers than with ideological debate. Their pragmatism, and a certain disdain they felt towards military repression (which meant that they were not easily intimidated) were other cultural traits that shaped the PT ethos.

The birth of the PT

Among the new union leaders was Luíz Inácio da Silva, known as Lula, a young man from a very poor family that had emigrated to São Paulo from the north-east). Lula immediately stood out because of his capacity to organise and unite the workers. In 1977 he led the ABC[7] metalworkers' campaign for increased wages and other benefits. Strikes exploded in the following year, first in São Bernardo and Diadema, and then throughout the state of São Paulo and some other regions; altogether 300 factories and 300,000 workers were involved. The strikes of May 1978 broke the military regime's repressive anti-strike laws and speeded up the end of the regime.

From the start, the new workers' leaders had two key guidelines: first, workers had to be autonomous; and second, strikes, even if successful, would never be enough to push through the reforms required to bring real improvements to the workers' lot. In December 1978, at a meeting convened by Lula, 14 activists, including 12 trade union leaders, talked seriously for the first time about creating a workers' political party. At first, only four of them approved the idea, but another three trade unionists soon joined them. In January 1979, the Ninth Metalworkers' Congress, held in Lins in the state of São Paulo, approved a proposal 'calling on all Brazilian workers to unite to build a party, the Workers' Party'.[8]

Events moved quickly. The following month the activists

published a 'Charter of Principles' in which they said that the problems of Brazilian society would not be overcome without the 'decisive participation of workers'. Two months later, on May Day, a national holiday in Brazil, they circulated the Workers' Party Charter, which stated that 'workers' emancipation must be achieved by workers themselves'. The military dictatorship was still very much alive, and the Charter added that 'democracy means organised and conscious participation by workers' in politics. In October of the same year, 130 supporters, attending a barbecue in São Bernardo, launched the 'movement for the Workers' Party' and elected a provisional national committee. On 10 February 1980, 1,200 people held a public meeting at Sion College in São Paulo and took the first steps towards formally creating the Workers' Party. Four months later, in June, driven on by a new wave of fiercely repressed strikes in the previous month, which had led to Lula's imprisonment by the government, the activists founded the new party, signing the manifesto and voting in favour of the statutes and the plan of action. Among the signatories were distinguished left-wingers and intellectuals, and the most representative leaders of the new unionism.[9]

The founding manifesto stated: 'The Workers' Party is born out of the workers' desire for political independence. They are tired of serving as electoral fodder for politicians and parties representing the current economic, social and political order…. Workers want to organise themselves as an autonomous political force.' The manifesto proclaimed that the PT was to be a mass party committed to full democracy exercised directly by the masses. 'Participation in elections and parliamentary activities will be subordinated to the objective of organising the exploited masses and their struggles.'[10] From the beginning the heterogeneous group that founded the PT, which included many who had earlier engaged in the armed struggle as well as Marxist groups and theoreticians, chose open democratic political debate, including participation in bourgeois political institutions, rather than revolution.

So, with the foundation of the PT, the Brazilian left, particularly those activists who were still licking their wounds from the failure of the Che Guevara-inspired cycle of armed struggle, opted for exclusively peaceful means for furthering the transition to democracy. The PT provided a political home for the activists who had survived armed struggle and exile, for the families of disappeared political prisoners and for various groups of activists and intellectuals who rejected Stalinism, especially the methods of the Brazilian Communist Party, and who had no desire to compromise with the dictatorship. Among the intellectuals and political activists were Mário Pedrosa, Brazil's best known art critic and a leading Trotskyist theoretician, Antônio Cândido, a famous literary critic, and Paulo Freire, who developed the pedagogy of liberation. These intellectuals and activists rejected the military leadership's offer of a limited political amnesty and a gradual and controlled return to democratic rule, an offer which was accepted by the *Movimento Democrático Brasileiro* (MDB), the main opposition party. The ABC strikes clearly put the case for full democracy and social change. The PT was at the heart of this agenda. But both the two traditional communist parties – the Soviet-line Brazilian Communist Party (Partido Comunista Brasileiro, PCB) and the former pro-Chinese and by now pro-Albanian Communist Party of Brazil (PCdoB) – immediately repudiated the PT's right to speak in the name of workers, and began to contest the new party's sphere of influence.

The new party also provoked important theoretical debates on the left, for it indirectly challenged the idea of compromise so widely accepted in Brazilian society. Until then, few political activists had contested the Brazilian Communist Party's view that Brazil was a dual society, in which the rule of a backward rural oligarchy, in alliance with imperialism, was being challenged by a new class of national industrialists. The solution, the PC argued, was to align with the industrialists in order to modernise Brazil. It was a dualist logic that took many forms: modernity versus backwardness; national bourgeoisie versus imperialism; capitalism versus feudalism. Even before the emergence of the PT, the dogma had already come under attack at a theoretical level. In 1962 an influential social scientist, Francisco de Oliveira, had written 'The Critique of Dualist Reason', an essay that had become the bible for all those exasperated with the dualist approach. He argued that backwardness was not in conflict with capitalism, but a necessary condition of it. If accepted, his argument destroyed the Communist Party's theoretical justification for the alliances it forged with modern capitalist groups. In founding the PT, a party created by and for the very class that the Communists claimed to be defending, Lula had provided a practical alternative to the Communist Party's multi-class strategy.

As intellectuals and exiled political leaders began to discuss Lula's idea of a Workers' Party, a split immediately appeared. Most intellectuals, including Almino Afonso, labour minister in the government of President João Goulart, which had been overthrown by the military in 1964, and Francisco Weffort, a political scientist who had written a highly influential essay on the collapse of populism, agreed that the 1978 and 1979 strikes had created a new working-class leadership and had been decisive in weakening the regime. Weffort also argued that, in a society still marked by an authoritarian culture and such a profound social imbalance that it was almost the continuation of slavery in disguised form, to achieve democracy was equivalent to staging a revolution. In this way he offered the left the last theoretical argument it needed in order to get rid of the old Marxist view of democracy as an instrument of class domination. In his view, democracy was a conquest of great strategic importance for the working classes and a process, rather than a rigid system, which has great counter-hegemonic potential. In fact, Weffort put into accepted neo-Marxist language what Lula and his fellow workers knew by instinct.

Even so, many intellectuals objected to the creation of a party that was class-oriented, arguing instead for a broad-based, democratic, socialist party. In particular, the influential sociologist, Fernando Henrique Cardoso, who had written extensively about dependent development and who had been forced into exile in the 1960s, strongly objected to the idea of such a party, claiming that this was tantamount to reducing social relations to labour relations. He also argued that the new unionists were falling into the trap set by the military government's new electoral law, which hoped to divide the opposition by encouraging a plethora of new parties. Cardoso doubted whether a party led by workers would recruit 10 per cent of the members of Congress, which was one of the conditions in the electoral law for the registration of new political parties.

Lula and the union leaders were undeterred. While welcoming into the party members of the opposition in Congress, they reiterated that workers would represent themselves directly in the new party and not be represented by others. Fernando Henrique Cardoso and Almino Afonso withdrew from the project, joining the only left-of-centre party permitted during the worst years of military rule, the MDB, later to be re-christened the Party of the Brazilian Democratic Movement (PMDB). Many members of the middle class shared Fernando Henrique Cardoso's view that workers by themselves did not have the knowledge to run a party, far less to govern the country.

But other important intellectuals, particularly those who had studied the Brazilian working class, joined the party. Among them were Francisco Weffort, the economist Paul Singer, the historian Marco Aurélio Garcia, the philosopher Marilena Chauí and the social scientist Florestan Fernandes. It was an impressive group. Some time later, after a crisis meeting within the MDB narrowed the options for its left-wing faction, several other members of Congress joined the party. Among them were Irma Passoni, a Catholic activist and one of the founding members of the Cost of Living Movement, which had got thousands into the streets in the 1970s in protest over the military's economic policy, the human rights lawyer Ayrton Soares, who had defended political prisoners, and the economist Eduardo Suplicy.

Some progressive intellectuals also rejected the idea of direct democracy inherent in the PT's documents. This idea, which is so difficult to implement in large democracies, reflected the radicalism of the founders of the PT, and, to some extent, their scepticism towards bourgeois political institutions. Obviously, the party entered the electoral game but throughout the twenty years of its existence the PT has made adherence to party decisions mandatory. It also imposed a duty on PT parliamentarians to contribute one third of their salaries – almost a punitive rate – to party coffers. However, these restrictions showed the electorate that the PT was a serious, principled party, different from the rest of Brazil's political parties, which made alliances whenever it suited their personal or group interests.

The party's tendencies

The coexistence of different tendencies within the PT was always problematic. This was partly because of the perverse logic involved, in which minority groups systematically joined each other to oppose the majority tendency and thus continually weakened the party, and partly because the consequent exacerbation of internal ideological debates made the party inward-looking and obstructed its dialogue with the masses.

In 1983, the leading group, including trade unionists around Lula, gave in to the reality of the tendencies and decided to become formally a tendency themselves. They called themselves *Articulação*, and it became the majority tendency within the PT. It was basically made up of trade union leaders, intellectuals and members of the old Aliança Libertadora Nacional (ALN), the armed struggle group created by Carlos Marighela, and was led by José Dirceu. Even now *Articulação*, which conceives of the PT as a mass party, open and democratic, effectively leads the party, sometimes in alliance with one group or another.

Tolerance of the tendencies was shaken in April 1986, when members of another breakaway faction of the Communist Party, the Brazilian Revolutionary Communist Party (PCBR), who were self-proclaimed PT members, were arrested after trying to rob a bank in the state of Bahia. One month later, the PT's Fourth National Conference approved a resolution that made adherence to the party's programme and discipline compulsory and banned dual party membership. The resolution defined the PT as a mass party, not an alliance of political organisations, nor an institutionalised front of the masses, (as alleged by some tendencies), which could 'be manipulated by any political party'.[11]

The following National Conference in 1988, which took place while the National Constituent Assembly was drawing up a new, democratic constitution (in which the PT and the mass movements played a decisive role), approved strict rules banning tendencies from having their own finances, leaders and papers. However, these rules were partially relaxed at the party's First Congress in 1991. In 1993, the PT expelled two Trotskyist groups that would not accept these restrictions – *Convergência Socialista* and *Causa Operária*.[12]

The fragmentation of the party into a large number of groups was one of the reasons for Lula's defeat in the 1994 presidential elections, although the main factor was undoubtedly the success of the anti-inflationary strategy known as the *Plano Real*. Responsibility for the organisation of the 1994 campaign was divided between factions, which meant that the campaign lacked unity. In various regions of the country, the tendencies made different tactical alliances to win a majority position in the PT.[13]

The party also became atomised, as personalist, sectoral and regional leaders exercised their influence and opposed any form of alliance with other left-of-centre parties, which were seen as 'populist'. However, after José Dirceu was elected to the

Table 1.1: Congressional Elections

Year	% votes for PT in the Chamber of Deputies	% of PT seats in in the Chamber	Number of PT seats	Number of PT senators
1982	3.5	1.7	8	0
1986	6.9	3.3	16	0
1990	10.2	7.0	37	1
1994	12.8	9.6	50	5
1998	13.2	11.3	60	8
2002	16.5	17.7	91	14

presidency of the party following Lula's electoral defeat in 1994, this resistance was worn down and the moderate tendencies – *Democracia Radical*, led by federal deputy José Genoíno, and *Articulação*, led by José Dirceu – became dominant. At the end of the decade, this so-called 'pragmatic' or 'majority' camp elected a third of the delegates to the Second Party Congress in Belo Horizonte in 1999.[14] Even so, the left of the party, gaining support from the deepening economic crisis, remained strong[15] and continued to support radical proposals, such as a moratorium on the foreign debt and the nationalisation of the banking system. José Dirceu was elected president of the party for three successive mandates.

Under the influence of Lula and José Dirceu the 1999 Congress approved a Programme for the Brazilian Democratic Revolution, which proposed a set of structural economic and political reforms within the framework of capitalism to be carried out, not by the PT alone, but by a wide coalition of forces. It is clearly a reformist programme, and its approval represented a serious defeat for the left-wing groups. Even so, the left-wing tendencies still have a profound impact on party life. The existence of the Marxist tendencies ensures that the PT continues to be a left-wing party, if not a Marxist one.

The strengths and weaknesses of the PT

The PT has been the main political beneficiary of the worsening Brazilian crisis, and especially of the failure of the bourgeois parties, but its progress has been uneven. In its first phase of growth, from its formation until the mid-1990s, civil society always demanded a great deal from the PT, usually more than it was able to deliver. In 1994, the PT went to the polls convinced that it could double its representation in Congress, just as it had managed in 1990, but to its bitter disappointment it did not achieve this. Even so, it increased the number of its federal deputies from 37 to 50, and its senators from one to five (see Table 1.1). The party was even more disappointed in the 1998 elections, when it grew at a slower rate (20 per cent), to 60 federal deputies and eight senators. This election signalled a temporary weakening of PT hegemony on the left, with the sudden growth of the small Brazilian Socialist Party (PSB). Some PT activists switched their allegiance to the PSB.

In part the PT's failure to realise its full electoral potential was due to its principled, or purist, political stance, which prevented it from making electoral promises it knew it could not deliver, or from using modern techniques of political marketing (although this was also the result of a scarcity of funds). The orthodox tendencies controlling regional branches of the PT also refused to make alliances with other parties or take other initiatives they considered opportunist. Moreover, the left as a whole continued to be hurt by the electoral system, inherited from the dictatorship, which was deliberately fashioned to favour conservative forces: under the rules of proportional representation, the state of São Paulo, where the PT is strong, should have 107 seats in the Federal Chamber of Deputies, but it has only 70; in contrast, small states in the north and north-east, where political patronage is common, should have only two or three seats but each has a statutory minimum of seven. Despite this, the PT made some inroads in the north-east, especially Bahia and Pernambuco, states with large populations that industrialised in the late 1990s. The PT also suffered from the rules on party political access to the media during elections, which the conservative majority periodically reformulated in its own favour.

Although PT expanded more slowly than it could have done, its growth was fast enough to leave big organisational and conceptual holes. As a result, the PT suffered significant setbacks and symbolic defeats, even in its home territory, the ABC industrial suburbs. In the second half of the 1990s, the PT gained the support of most state employees, but did not manage to communicate with workers in the huge informal sector of the economy or with the middle classes. At the end of the 1990s, unemployment almost doubled. The PT should have benefited greatly, but it lost power among workers and did not manage to maintain its appeal to young university students, who traditionally have formed a significant proportion of Latin America's political activists but at this period became seduced by neo-liberal ideas. Because of these failures, state employees increased their relative influence within the movement. As they were being hit hard by neo-liberalism at the time, with changes in the labour law and higher rates of unemployment, the PT became caught up in their struggle. It also found it difficult to create a public debate around alternatives, as it was still boycotted by the media. As a result, the PT was unable to react adequately to the big wave of privatisations undertaken by the Cardoso government. It failed to challenge neo-liberal ideas successfully or to formulate policies that would appeal to society as a whole.

Along with neo-liberalism, political patronage, populism and corruption have remained the PT's main external enemies. Corruption and right-wing populism were responsible for the defeat of the PT candidate for the governorship of Brasília both in 1998 and again in 2002. The PT's main internal weakness continues to be infighting. In the 1998 elections, the PT won the elections for state governor in Acre and Mato Grosso do Sul, as well as in Rio Grande do Sul, but it lost Espírito Santo, the first state it had ever governed, and Brasília, in both cases largely as a result of internal party struggles. Once again, in 2002, internal bickering largely accounted for the PT's main electoral disappointment – the failure to hold on to Rio Grande do Sul. The exacerbation of internal struggles at a regional level, precisely at the moment when the party has been changing from an assortment of factions into a mass party, has been a recurring feature of the party's setbacks.

The PT in local government

Right from its first victory in 1982 in the municipal elections in Diadema, a poor region in the ABC industrial belt, the PT began to establish a record of innovative local administrations. It became a trademark of the PT's local administrations to give priority to public health, housing and education. These policies were often successful, and in Diadema, for instance, the PT was returned to office three times. However, a few of its other early experiments in local power were more problematic. In 1985 Maria Luisa Fontenelle was unexpectedly elected mayor of Fortaleza, the capital of Ceará, giving the PT its first victory in a state capital. As Margaret Keck has shown, the peculiar dynamics of the Brazilian political system made the PT the ideal vehicle for the protest vote, the 'last hope for change' for desperate voters. But the PT administration was not a success. Fontenelle belonged to a Maoist faction within the PT and did not receive the support of the rest of the party. She was also viciously attacked by local businessmen and landowners.

In 1988 the PT leapt to national prominence, in particular when the party rather unexpectedly won the mayoral elections in several large state capitals including Brazil's largest city, São Paulo, which has over 10 million inhabitants (a third of whom live in precarious conditions in shanty-towns) and a chaotic public transport system. But the São Paulo PT administration was a traumatic experience. The mayor, Luiza Erundina, an energetic social worker, had to fight all sorts of boycotts, including one organised by unions and another by the local party branch. She, too, made mistakes but, in the end, the PT managed to make some real advances. Even so, the experience left a bitter aftertaste for many of those involved, and Erundina eventually left the PT.

In 2000 PT mayors were re-elected in Porto Alegre and Belém and the party's candidates were also successful in São Paulo, Recife, Aracaju and Goiânia. In coalitions with other parties, it elected mayors in Belo Horizonte and Macapá. In these elections, it received 11.9 million votes (14.13 per cent of the total) and came to power in cities with an aggregate population of 28.8 million people, four times more than it was governing in 1996.

Slowly the PT established a good administrative record elsewhere, particularly in Santos and in Porto Alegre (see Chapter 4). In Santos, a port with over one million inhabitants, the two PT mayors – first, Telma de Souza and then David Capistrano – introduced innovative solutions for public health and sanitation problems. They cleaned up the pollution on the beaches and introduced an advanced experiment in psychiatric reform, closing the city's largest asylum and restoring the rights of many mentally ill citizens by returning them to their communities. They also adopted courageous polices to fight AIDS, and repaired the drainage system, built at the beginning of the century to fight yellow fever. By 1992 the PT was in power in four state capitals and 50 medium-sized or large cities, generally inhabited by large numbers of industrial workers. As well as the city of São Paulo, it governed such important cities in São Paulo state as São José dos Campos, Campinas, Londrina and Ribeirão Preto, each with about one million inhabitants.

After Lula's defeat in the 1994 presidential elections, the PT national leadership began to place more value on gaining experience by governing the large number of municipalities under its control and the two states – Federal District (Brasília) and

Table 1.2: Municipal Elections

Year	Number of mayors	Number of councillors
1982	2	127
1988	37	1006
1992	54	1100
1996	115	1895
2000	174	2475

Table 1.3: State Elections

Year	Number of governors	Number of state deputies
1982	0	12
1986	0	40
1990	0	81
1994	2	92
1998	3	90
2002	3	147

Espírito Santo – where it had elected governors. A special secretariat was created by the national leadership to accompany and help local governments. Slowly but steadily, the PT managed to establish a reputation for honesty, innovation and commitment to the interests of the population in local and state governments. Honesty emerged as a determining factor in increasing the party's prestige.

Santo André, one of the towns in the ABC industrial belt where Lula began his political career, was the main laboratory for the PT's administrative innovations. The basis of the municipality's plans was the concept of 'social inclusion'. Almost all projects and development plans were directed towards the improvement of the social conditions of the underprivileged and their inclusion in society as active citizens.

Specific programmes were created for each of the main social problems: a family doctor service to improve the health service; a literacy programme for young people and adults; a programme for guaranteeing a minimum family income; a bank for providing loans for lower-income groups; a training programme for small-businessmen; a low-cost housing programme; an urbanisation programme for shanty-towns; and so on. The Santo André administration was repeatedly re-elected many times and won several prizes, including the Getúlio Vargas Foundation and Ford Foundation prizes as the country's best municipal administration.

Santo André became an example throughout the country of how a municipal administration could be run on socially responsible lines. The conservative elite was quick to understand the political potential of this image and mayors from other political parties, even some conservative ones, began here and there to adopt similar policies. But at the same time corruption and organised crime also reached new levels, as the economic crisis worsened, and this damaged the image of the conservative camp, particularly when drug trafficking groups were found to have infiltrated high echelons of the state administration, as happened in Goiás, São Paulo, Rio de Janeiro, Mato Grosso, Espírito Santo and Alagoas. PT politicians began to be targeted by criminal gangs, and two mayors, including Celso Daniel, the mayor of Santo André, who would undoubtedly have played a key role in the Lula government, were killed.

In the Amazon region, the PT played an outstanding role in the development of so-called 'extractive reserves' (that is, large protected areas of the tropical forest where only sustainable activities, such as rubber-tapping, are permitted) in the state of Acre in the west of the Amazon basin. The man behind this project was the rubber-tapper leader Chico Mendes, who set up the PT in Xapuri, a small town in the Amazon forest. In December 1988 Chico Mendes was murdered by ranchers, but eventually in 1998 Jorge Viana, who had earlier been a successful mayor of the state capital, Rio Branco, was elected governor (and re-elected in 2002, even though his campaign against organised crime provoked fierce opposition). In the Federal District, Brasília, the former Chancellor of the University of Brasília, Cristovam Buarque, who was elected governor in 1994 (and has become Minister of Education in the Lula government), came across the innovative *bolsa-escola* (school grant) programme, first conceived by a PSDP mayor in Campinas, by which a benefit was paid to all families on low incomes who sent their children to school. Cristovam Buarque very successfully introduced an expanded version of the programme in Brasília. It was adopted, with some modifications, by other local authorities, and then applied on a national scale (though with insufficient resources) by President Fernando Henrique Cardoso.

The parliamentary experience

Although for twenty years the PT had a relatively small number of seats in Congress, it played a decisive role in parliamentary proceedings. Its most important contributions came in the Constituent Assembly in 1988, when it helped to block anti-democratic proposals for the new constitution, and then in 1993 when, soon after President Fernando Collor de Mello was forced out of office, it uncovered a huge corruption scam in what became known as the 'budget scandal'. The PT federal deputies José Genoíno, Aloízio Mercadante and Hélio Bicudo, and the senator, Eduardo Suplicy, regularly receive huge votes in the elections. Whereas the parliamentary representatives of other parties are often accused of corruption, such a charge is rarely made against the PT, which has strengthened its reputation as an ethical party. PT's federal deputies are routinely found at the top of the lists of best representatives in Congress regularly produced by some newspapers.

In comparison with other parties, the PT is still the party with by far the largest number of elected representatives from the working class and the liberal professions. Two-thirds of the party's congressional representatives have links with trade unions or other social movements. The first women ever elected to the Senate were PT candidates: Benedita da Silva, who still lives in a shanty-town in Rio de Janeiro, was the first black woman to take a seat in Congress; and Marina da Silva (see profile below) comes from a family of rubber-tappers in Acre.

Profile: Maria Osmarina Silva de Souza

The life story of Marina, as she is universally known, is a remarkable demonstration of the opportunities that the PT has already opened up for excluded Brazilians. Born into a poor family of rubber-tappers in the Amazon state of Acre, she learnt to read and write when she was 16 years old and, after a meteoric political career, was elected to an eight-year term as senator in October 1994. Aged 38, she was the youngest person to be elected senator in the history of Brazil. In October 2002 Marina was re-elected. She has become Minister of the Environment in the Lula government

In February 1958 Marina was born in a hut made out of the trunks of palm trees and standing on poles to protect it from the seasonal river floods, on an isolated rubber plantation 70 km from Rio Branco, the capital of Acre. The rubber-tappers and their families received little medical assistance, for a lengthy river journey separated them from the outside world. Marina's parents had 11 children but, without medical assistance, three died as babies. Marina recalls, 'I saw electric light for the first time when I was taken by river to Rio Branco to receive treatment for poisoning caused by a remedy for worms. I still remember the amazement I felt seeing a Christmas tree decorated with fairy lights.'

When she was about five, her family moved to the city of Manaus on the Amazon river, where they set up a small store. But the shop went bankrupt in five months, and they all travelled by boat, sleeping in hammocks, to the mouth of the river. There they planted cassava to make manioc flour, but again the initiative failed. Marina's father got in touch with the owner of the rubber plantation back in Acre, and he agreed to pay for them to go back, provided that the family paid off the debt by producing extra rubber. Still just ten years old, Marina used to get up at five in the morning every day of the week, to make the 14 km trek through the forest with her father and elder sister, first to slit the trunks of the rubber trees and then to collect the latex. They paid off the debt. Like other members of her family, Marina was often ill, suffering from five attacks of malaria and two bouts of hepatitis.

When Marina was 15 years old, two of her sisters died within a fortnight, one from malaria and the other from measles. Six months later her mother died from a stroke. She begged her father to let her go to Rio Branco to realise her two dreams: to study and to become a nun. Marina said later. 'It was the most important moment of my life. My father said yes and I left the plantation. I first stepped into a school when I was 16 years old.'

Despite her late start, Marina proved an excellent student. By the time she was 26, she had graduated in history at the University of Acre, financing her studies by working as a maid. By then she had given up the idea of being a nun, 'I realised that I would have to repress all my sexuality and that wasn't the right option for me', and had married. Partly through her participation in base Christian communities, she became politicised. She took part in *empates*, acts of civil resistance, organised by the renowned rubber-tapper Chico Mendes, during which whole communities of rubber-tappers stopped the tractors sent in by cattle-ranchers to clear the forest. She helped Chico Mendes to set up a local branch of the CUT.

Her husband disapproved of her growing involvement in politics, and eventually they separated. Marina says that it was a difficult decision for her, because by then she had two children and was still deeply religious. She eventually married again and had two more children. In 1988, shortly before Chico Mendes was murdered by a cattle-rancher, she was elected to the municipal council. With her dark Afro-Indian skin and long, curly black hair, Marina, like so many of the region's other inhabitants, is of mixed ethnic origins.

In 1990, she was elected state deputy, obtaining the largest number of votes ever recorded in Acre.

She was very active as a deputy, but in 1991 was taken seriously ill. PT friends helped to fly her down to São Paulo, but no doctor could discover what was wrong with her. She recalls, 'I felt a strange taste on my tongue, as if I had put a coin in my mouth; I told everyone that I was suffering from metal poisoning, but the medical tests showed nothing.' Eventually Marina found a specialist in the field who confirmed her suspicions. The specialist believes that her heavy-metal contamination was caused by the strong medicine she received for malaria attacks when she still lived in the forest. She has responded to treatment, but has to be very careful what she eats, avoiding all processed foods.

During her eight years as a senator, Marina was extremely active, responsible for numerous initiatives to protect biodiversity and to stop biopiracy. When another *petista*, Jorge Viana, was elected governor of Acre in 1998, she was able to work closely with him to develop a series of sustainable development projects in consultation with NGOs and forest dwellers, and with a US$100 million loan from the InterAmerican Development Bank (IDB).

The PT and the mass movements

Ever since it was founded, the PT has viewed itself not as a conventional political party, but as the nucleus of a network of popular movements. This relationship is strategically important for the PT, because it forms part of its conception of political power. Influenced by Gramsci, it believes in the gradual conquest of political space and the construction of popular hegemony.[15] It was in this spirit that it undertook many important initiatives. In 1981 PT cadres created the CUT in an attempt to gain hegemony in the trade union movement. It also backed a little-known movement for better health care that had a decisive influence in the creation of the Sistema Único de Saúde (the Universal Health System, SUS), which is Brazil's public health system today. In 1983 it launched the *Diretas Já*

(Direct Elections Now) campaign, which captured the hearts and minds of young people and rapidly became the most important public movement for the restoration of full democracy since the 1964 military coup (even though the right to elect the president by direct vote was only reinstated in 1989, six years later), while simultaneously staging (also in 1989) the most important national strike in more than 20 years.

Meanwhile, the PT's Agriculture Secretariat, headed by José Gomes da Silva, one of the party's main thinkers, kept the debate about land reform alive, and this issue became one of the party's priorities. Some of the leaders of the MST, which was founded in Rio Grande do Sul in 1984 by activists linked to the Catholic Church's Pastoral Land Commission (CPT) were also PT activists. The MST became the most active social movement in Brazil in the late 1990s, when structural unemployment weakened the trade union movement and encouraged unemployed people to join the MST. Most of the participants in the single-issue social movements (which are a feature of Brazilian society) are also active in the PT and the Catholic Church. The PT even has a big presence in more recent movements instigated by the urban middle classes, such as some of the environmental non-governmental organisations. It is perhaps not surprising that most of the bills in Congress that are of interest to the mass movements are put forward by the PT.

However, the PT has always found it difficult to transform local grassroots campaigns into successful national movements, despite the success of some protest marches jointly organised by social movements, such as *O Grito dos Excluídos* (the Cry of the Excluded) led by the Catholic Church every year on 7 September (a national holiday to commemorate the Declaration of Independence from Portugal in 1822). There are various reasons for this: the wish of the local movements to remain autonomous, the PT's culture of not co-opting such movements, and the ability of centre and right-wing parties, not constrained by the PT's scruples, to intervene at critical moments. It is

Table 1.4: Lula's Record in the Presidential Elections

Year	1st round: votes	1st round: % of votes	2nd round: votes	2nd round: % of votes
1989	11,622,000	16.0	31,000,000	44.2
1994	16,802,000	22.0	—	—
1998	21,803,000	26.1	—	—
2002	39,444,000	46.4	57,200,000	61.3

Note: The figures refer to valid votes cast.

interesting to note that, although the PT launched the *Diretas Já* campaign for direct presidential elections in 1983, it immediately lost control of it to the liberals.

In 1991, two years after being defeated by Collor de Mello in his first attempt to become President (see Table 1.4), Lula set up an informal 'parallel government', inspired by the British Labour Party's Shadow Cabinet of the time. This 'parallel government' began to discuss alternative policies and the demands of the mass movement, as well as the country's macro-economic situation. Out of this emerged Brazil's most important attempt so far to fight hunger, the Emergency Food Programme, which associated the fight against hunger with land reform and the redistribution of income in rural areas. This programme, which captured the imagination of the country, was led by Herbert de Souza, universally known as *Betinho*. He was a courageous and charismatic social campaigner and a haemophiliac who later died from AIDS. The government eventually adopted the programme, but reduced it to a merely charitable operation involving only the distribution of food.

Immediately afterwards, Lula set up the *Instituto Cidadania* (Citizenship Institute), a kind of NGO dedicated to formulating alternative government policies. As Lula ran this institute himself, he was able to invite into it the people he wanted, without directly involving the party. With the support of other NGOs, the Citizenship Institute first formulated a policy on housing, aimed at resolving Brazil's serious problem of homelessness, which is considered to be the most comprehensive study of its kind in Brazil. It then started a project called *Zero Fome* (Zero Hunger) with the aim of ending hunger in Brazil, before eventually looking at the question of public safety, with a view to tackling the roots of the problem of urban violence. Those involved in the Citizenship Institute – activists, party workers, trade unionists and political leaders – are largely party members who are aligned with Lula or people from outside who have been touched by his charisma.

The PT has a National Mass Movements Secretariat and, along with other left-wing parties, it created the National Forum of Democratic and Popular Organisations in an attempt to promote links between the different parts of the social movement and to involve smaller parties within the PT's orbit. The PT's most direct influence has been on the trade union movement, since the CUT, which was created by the PT, has become the dominant trade union force. Several former CUT leaders are now PT Congressional representatives. At the end of the 1990s, unemployment doubled, becoming particularly severe in the trade union organisation's main area of influence, São Paulo, and the CUT's influence diminished a great deal, while the influence of its main rival, *Força Sindical*, increased with the support of employers and the government. However, CUT is still strong, for it is backed by state employees, industrial workers and, since the beginning of the 1990s, agricultural labourers.

The strongest mass movement at the end of the 1990s, the MST, competes with the PT for political space, despite their intimate relationship and ideological affinities. The MST has a much broader and more ambitious political programme than land reform, the issue that led to its creation. It supports the PT in election campaigns and is, in turn, supported by the PT. But it has its own firmly left-wing political programme, which originated in Catholic liberation theology (in which the PT also has roots). Activists study Marx and Lenin in Che Guevara schools, and the MST's strongly moralistic programme proposes confiscating wealth from the richest, a moratorium on the foreign debt and changes in patterns of consumption as necessary for a redistribution of income.

The PT provides decisive support for land reform and regards this issue as a priority. It has organised several campaigns to protest against violence in rural areas and the assassination of rural leaders, many of them also PT leaders. It does not, however, endorse the MST's political programme. There was a moment during the 1998 presidential elections when the PT tried to change what had been until then a conventional electoral campaign into a kind of mass social movement, because it was felt that Lula would not be elected without the backing of a strong popular movement, or, if elected with a small majority, would be unable to govern. After Lula's defeat in 1998 the discussion about links between the PT, the MST, CUT and other smaller social movements was taken up again, with a view to forming a bloc capable of disputing political hegemony with neo-liberalism.

The idea was that a PT presidential candidate would be elected only on the back of a strong, well-organised protest campaign that would be able to channel dissatisfaction, put an end to prejudice and break with traditional political practice. As it turned out, however, the deepening of the crisis made this approach unnecessary and even risky. The PT adopted a new strategy, in which it sought to win over the centre of the political spectrum and not to alienate conservatives. As a result, it decided deliberately to create space between the party and the social movements, opting, for instance, not to participate officially in the second referendum on the foreign debt held by the Catholic Church and a dozen other organisations, although its militants were free to join as individuals. It also got a commitment from the MST not to carry out land occupations during the campaign or carry out any other acts that could be exploited by the right wing to undermine Lula's candidacy. In a controversial decision that alarmed some of its most committed activists, it also formed an alliance with the right-of-centre Liberal Party.

The PT's coming to power completely changes its relationship with social movements. To some extent, this has happened at the local level after the PT has won an election, when the PT administration and public employees have agreed to establish relations at a strategic level in which they both see each other as partners in a much broader social and political project. It has been agreed that specific demands, such as a demand by public employees or teachers for a wage increase, must be negotiated with the mutual understanding that resources are limited. But this arrangement does not always work satisfactorily, if for no other reason than that in many situations the local union is under the control of a PT faction that is struggling for more power within the party or the municipality structure. Now that the PT has won the national elections, it will face a much larger challenge in dealing with the expectations of popular movements and unions. The idea that relations must be established at a strategic level of interest remains valid, but the scope for problems and potential conflicts is much greater.

The problem of socialism

Although it has never defined a precise socialist doctrine, the PT claims to be a socialist party and, although it never called itself Marxist, its behaviour in some ways is typical of Marxist parties.[17] At its Fifth National Conference in 1987, it began the delicate discussion of what type of socialism the party stood for. It stated that 'the conquest of socialism and the construction of a socialist society' are 'the main strategic objectives of the Workers' Party'. Although it did not say at this conference that the party was the only instrument open to workers in their struggle, the PT still used the jargon of an elementary interpretation of Marxism and history to express itself. At its Seventh National Conference in June 1990, it passed a resolution that stated that the PT did not believe socialism was possible without democracy: 'either our socialism will be radically democratic or it will not be socialism at all'. The discussion continued in 1991 at the party's First Congress, in which left-wing leaders from all of Latin America participated. The Berlin Wall had just fallen. The party recognised that

> the collapse of the regimes in eastern Europe, together with the crisis in the USSR and the other countries in the so-called socialist bloc, does not only represent the twilight of Stalinism and totalitarianism, posing as socialism. In a certain sense, what we are living through is the dismantling of a large part of what the international socialist workers' movement has constructed since the Russian Revolution in October 1917. ... [W]e have to recognise that we are witnessing the end of the cycle of socialist revolutions begun with the Russian Revolution in 1917 and the model of society that they inspired....

However, the PT did not manage to change as quickly as its own analysis required. Despite the growth in its electoral support, the number of its activists declined and many of those that remained were enlisted to help run municipal and state government administrations or to represent the party politically. Moreover, the increase in social exclusion meant that workers with formal employment contracts and state employees – natural supporters of the PT – became part of what could be seen in the Brazilian context as a privileged elite. This made it particularly difficult for the PT to formulate policies that could appeal both to them and the excluded masses. While neoliberalism attracted middle-class yuppies and others away from the PT, the MST increasingly became a magnet for the excluded and unemployed.

As early as the First Party Congress in 1991, the PT had recognised the new factors at play on the world stage – the vigour of large-scale capital and the United States; the importance of the technological revolution and its potential for changing the nature of industrial work; and the neo-liberal attack on the social gains made by workers over the decades. All these factors came together to bring down further the level of capitalist development in Latin America, a region that on the eve of a new millennium was already weighed down by its foreign debt, drug trafficking and structural unemployment:

> The historic impasse of capitalism in the region and the inability of neo-liberalism and the elites to find solutions means that the left must come up with an emergency development plan ... and must build an alternative development model based on democratic and libertarian socialist ideas ... a new economic, legal and ecological order that has as its fundamental demand the democratisation of power.[19]

At the following Congress eight years later, the ideas defended by the various PT tendencies reflected a stronger feeling that socialist ideas had suffered a major defeat at the international level, and even greater perplexity at the increase in structural unemployment and the renewed vigour of capitalism. They also reflected the perception that the party urgently needed to develop a new political discourse directed towards new sectors of the mass population, other than industrial workers and state employees, and a clearer perception of how to make national alliances in order to achieve power.

The destruction in the late 1990s of what was left of the national bourgeoisie by Fernando Henrique Cardoso's neo-liberal policies and its replacement by a new elite, aligned with transnational capital, significantly reduced the range of alliances open to the PT. On the other hand, the pauperisation of the middle classes and the general deterioration in the country's social fabric, and even in the material base of the country, especially its forests and its cities, opened up the possibility of a new alliance founded on ethical and ecological – as much as ideological and political – values.

As it turned out, Lula's manifesto for the 2002 campaign, *Carta ao povo brasileiro* (Letter to the Brazilian people), was a strong commitment to getting the country growing again and to create jobs, but it fell short of being a new paradigm for sustainable development and was on some points confusingly vague. It also contained a commitment 'not to break contracts', which is a euphemism for not declaring a moratorium on foreign and domestic debts, a tactical concession that became necessary in view of the extremely aggressive attitudes adopted by the international banks in their campaign against his candidacy.

The strategy that led to Lula's victory

Lula's strategy to win the presidency was drawn up almost immediately after his defeat in the 1998 election campaign, when he ran only to serve the party, knowing full well that he did not stand a chance. When asked to consider standing again for the fourth time Lula imposed conditions, even before his nomination was official. This time, he said, he was going to be a candidate only if the party gave him a free hand to establish alliances and to employ the technical and human resources needed to achieve victory. This time he wanted to win. He was not going to run for the sake of running, or merely to help the PT elect members of Congress and state governors, as he had done in 1998.

In consultation with the party's president, José Dirceu, he drew up a strategy to isolate the left wing of the party. They got the 1999 Congress to pass a 'Programme for the Brazilian Democratic Revolution', which stated that the revolution would be achieved around three pillars – the social, the democratic and the national – and that it would be carried out not by the PT alone but by a wide coalition of forces. It was this programme that paved the way for Lula to formulate his successful strategy for the 2002 presidential campaign. This Congress, in fact, gave Lula *carte blanche* to form whatever alliance of forces he wished, in order to increase the chances of victory.

As part of this strategy, the party organised a very effective centralised campaign for the 2000 municipal elections. It established national rules, formulated slogans, prepared a coherent 'message', and edited campaign materials that allowed it to overcome the internal problems caused by factionalism. Lula was the leader of this campaign, staging mass meetings all over the country. Although he was not a candidate, he appeared in all regional and national television broadcasts. As a result, the PT inflicted a major defeat on the conservative political parties, winning a large number of towns in Bahia, Santa Catarina and Paraná, traditionally strongholds of political patronage

Following the 2000 landslide, Lula intensified his activities in his Citizenship Institute, from where he began to coordinate a series of working groups on the country's main problems, particularly housing, infrastructure, employment and agriculture. Well before the start of the electoral campaign, the Institute gathered together NGOs and some of the country's leading experts and drew up comprehensive proposals to tackle some of the country's main social problems, such as unemployment, urban violence and lack of housing. It also organised public meetings with the business community, attended by a leading sugar-cane and alcohol producers' association and three state governors, and held a round table on poverty with the support of the governor of Bahia, Antônio Carlos Magalhães, the leader of Brazilian conservatives and a symbol of reactionary politics. In effect, Lula was signalling, in particular to the party cadres, that the time had come for a policy of wide alliances and dialogue. The Institute was a particularly suitable base for the move, as it provided a space for debate free from the party's internal power disputes.

However, it was at the insistence of another politician, Senator Suplicy, who also wanted to become the party's presidential candidate, that the party was forced to stage, for the first time in Brazil, primary party elections with the direct voting of all party members, a decision that almost upset Lula's plans. Though Lula was reluctant to compete with another party candidate for nomination, he decided in the end to allow his name to be put forward. Without actually campaigning, Lula ended up with about 70 per cent of the votes.

A clear strategy was then drawn up to win over the centre of the political spectrum in the presidential campaign. An analysis of Lula's three previous defeats had shown that Lula and the PT had a captive vote of almost one third of the electorate, but was also firmly rejected by another third of the electorate. The only way of winning was by getting the support of the one third of undecided voters who came mainly from the middle classes and the less educated workers. So Lula and his aides decided, much to the astonishment of the bourgeoisie, to hire the country's leading expert in political propaganda and to form a modern press office. Together, they worked out the best discourse for combating prejudice and raising people's hope for a better future. However, Lula never made specific and unrealistic promises, as a populist politician would have done.

It was Lula's fourth attempt to gain the presidency, and, along with the familiar criticism of the party for being too left-wing, critics still attacked Lula for his 'lack of formal educa-tion', a euphemism for his humble background. It expressed the refusal of the ruling elite to accept that someone from the working class was fit to rule the country. More than ideological resistance to a left-wing party, it was the class factor at work, in a society shaped by nearly four hundred years of slavery. The media encouraged these ideas, which echoed the rejection of worker autonomy by left-wing intellectuals, led by Fernando Henrique Cardoso, at around the time of the creation of the PT, and which were nurtured by the low self-esteem of a population long used to being dominated.

The class argument was disguised in various ways in the 2002 campaign, but it was not abandoned. Most of the press, and even some educated social scientists, repeatedly criticised Lula for his alleged 'lack of knowledge' or, more subtly, 'lack of administrative experience'. Lula patiently refuted the argu-ments and, by waging an extremely competent campaign in which the main slogan was 'Brazil must change', showed that the charge of incompetence was completely unfounded. He proved that competence must be political, not technical, and showed himself to be the only candidate prepared to negotiate a wide social pact to take Brazil out of its crisis. He went so far as to organise round-table discussions with sectors such as bankers and landowners, which used to see him as an enemy to be defeated. Slowly at first but steadily, the argument of incompetence began to work in the opposite direction: instead of fuelling prejudice against Lula, as in previous campaigns, it angered people. So his adversaries, in particular the ruling party, the PSDB, tried to exploit people's fear by comparing Brazil's crisis with Argentina's: so, in the end, it became a campaign of those who hoped against those who feared. And, as Lula's slogan put it, in the end 'hope defeated fear'.

Notes

1 Margaret E Keck, *The Workers' Party and Democratization in Brazil*, Yale University Press, New Haven, 1991.
2 The main groups that joined the PT were: Socialist Democracy (*Democracia Socialista*), a Trotskyist group, affiliated to the Fourth International, which wanted to transform the PT into a revolutionary Marxist party; Socialist Convergence (*Convergência Socialista*), also Trotskyist, which aimed to transform the PT into a mass Marxist party; the small group, Movement for the Emancipation of the Proletariat (*Movimento de Emancipação do Proletariado – MEP*); the PCBR (split from the PCdoB) and the APML, both of which saw the PT as a transitional party and a recruiting ground; *Libelu*, a fraction of the Fourth International, which aimed to take control of the new party.
3 The Workers' Party, *Resoluções de Encontros e Congressos* (Conference and Congress Resolutions) (editora Fundação Perseu Abramo), São Paulo, 1998.
4 Emir Sader, *Quando novos personagens entram em cena*, Paz e Terra, São Paulo, 1988.
5 Including Frei Betto, Plínio de Arruda Sampaio and Irma Passoni.
6 *Pelego* is the cowhide that horsemen put underneath the saddle to absorb the impact caused when horse and rider are in motion or, as it is used here, to stop it rubbing a sore patch on the horse's skin.
7 ABC is the name given to the industrial belt outside São Paulo, made up of the municipal districts of Santo André, São Bernardo and São Caetano.
8 Known as the Thesis of Lins. For this and other documents about the history of the PT, see Conference and Congress Resolutions.

9 Among the founders and first leaders of the party were Apolônio de Carvalho, Mario Pedrosa, Manoel da Conceição, Sergio Buarque de Holanda, Moacyr Gadotti, Antônio Cândido, Florestan Fernandes, Paul Singer, Francisco Weffort, José Ibrahim, Helena Greco and Paulo Freire.

10 Conference and Congress Resolutions.

11 Ibid.; PT Political Action and Organisational Plan 1986–88 (*Plano de Ação Política e Organizativa do PT para o período 1986–88*). São Paulo, Editora Fundação Perseu Abramo, 1998.

12 *Convergencia Socialista* formed its own party, the Unified Socialist Workers' Party (*Partido Socialista dos Trabalhadores Unificado – PSTU*), which supported Lula in the 1994 campaign.

13 The main tendencies on the eve of the 1994 campaign were: Left Choice (*Opção à esquerda*) (33 per cent), formed by *Democracia Socialista* and members of the ALN such as Ruy Falcão; Unity in Struggle (*Unidade na Luta*) (31 per cent), formed by trade union leaders such as Lula and Olívio Dutra; In the Struggle (*Na Luta*) (20 per cent), orthodox Marxist tendency formed by Sokol and Greenhalgh; *Democracia Radical* (11 per cent), parliamentary social democrats, formed by Eduardo Jorge and José Genoíno; and independents, such as Francisco Weffort and other intellectuals.

14 *Articulação* elected 33 per cent of delegates. The PT in Struggle (*Na Luta PT*) group, formed by the Trotskyist group Labour (*O Trabalho*) and deputy Luis Eduardo Greenhalgh, elected 20 per cent of delegates. The party began to be run jointly by these tendencies. To the right, the Radical Democracy (*Democracia radical*), formed mainly by members of Congress, elected only 11 per cent of delegates; other tendencies and independents elected the remaining delegates.

15 The main ones were *Democracia Socialista*, affiliated to Mandel's Fourth International; Redoing (*Refazendo*), led by the Rio de Janeiro federal deputy, Milton Temer; and Network (*Rede*), led by the ex-mayor of Porto Alegre, Tarso Genro, who was considered a possible PT presidential candidate. Other groups, such as *O Trabalho*, continued to exist.

16 A resolution at the party's First Congress spoke of the 'need to build a broad network of social and popular movements; to permit the combination of the most varied forms of struggle and links between urban and rural areas; and the construction of a political and social bloc and the dispute of hegemony'. Conference and Congress Resolutions, pp. 479 ff.

17 All routine political decisions are voted on by the 21 members of the National Executive Commission, which meets regularly. More important decisions go to meetings of the 86-member National Directorate. Strategic or ideological issues are discussed in Conferences, held every two years, or at Congress, held every five years. Congress has the same rigorous format as the major socialist parties had at the beginning of the twentieth century.

18 Conference and Congress Resolutions, pp. 479 ff.

19 Ibid.

2
The Making of
a Leader

SUE BRANFORD

When the PT was founded in 1980, the freshness of its vision won the support of thousands of young industrial workers who had been brought up under the military dictatorship, when left-wing parties were banned. Bombarded by pro-government propaganda on the television and radio, the vast majority of these workers did not define themselves as left-wing, let alone socialist; most of them probably adhered to the practice, widespread at the time, of using the word *comunista* as a routine word of abuse. But they knew what they wanted: better wages, better working conditions, greater political freedom, and the right to reorganise their trade union movement so that it would truly represent their interests.

Lula quickly emerged as the leader of this new labour movement. Lula is a born leader with a remarkable capacity to captivate an audience. Factory workers will happily stand for half an hour or more, in the hot sun or pouring rain, listening to him. He thinks well on his feet and speaks from the heart, as he explained in an interview in 1994:

> I don't know if it is a weakness or not, but, to speak frankly, I often prefer to rely on my intuition than to work things out in my head. I think that intuition lets you put a bit of your heart in things, and I think to do politics without your heart makes people very hard, very realistic. And I don't think that's good in politics. I don't think that you can be a good politician without deep human feelings, and I don't want to lose that side of me.[1]

54

Brazil's industrial workers feel an immediate affinity with Lula who, until he became a national figure, had lived a life much like their own. He was born, probably on 27 October 1945 (the exact date on which he was to be elected President 57 years later) in Caetés in the municipal district of Garanhuns in the poor north-eastern state of Pernambuco. His parents were impoverished subsistence peasants and Lula was the seventh of eight children. Shortly after he was born, his father, like hundreds of thousands of others from the north-east, made the long journey south to the state of São Paulo, in search of work. He got a job in the docks in the port of Santos, loading bags of coffee. The first time Lula remembers seeing his father was when he came back to visit the family, when Lula was five years old.

Back in Pernambuco, Lula's mother, Eurídice Ferreira de Mello, struggled to feed and educate her children. Often they went to bed hungry. Overwhelmed by the effort, Lula's mother decided in December 1952 to leave the north-east and, with her eight children, to join her husband in São Paulo state. The 3,000 km journey in the back of an open lorry took them 13 days. At first, the family went to live with the father in Vicente de Carvalho, a poor neighbourhood in the seaside resort of Guarujá, near the port of Santos. To boost the family income, Lula, aged seven, sold peanuts, tapioca and oranges in the streets.

But the reunion between Lula's parents did not work out. Like so many other Brazilian men, Lula's father had started living with another woman – in fact, a cousin to his first wife – during the years he was separated from his first family. For a while Lula's father tried to juggle the two families, but in 1956 Eurídice decided she had had enough and moved with her children to São Paulo city. Partly perhaps because he never knew his father properly, Lula developed a very close and warm relationship with his mother. Even today he refers frequently to his mother's pride and happiness when he finally got his technical diploma, and his regret that she did not live long enough to see him elected President. It is an experience with which many poor Brazilian men and women can identify, in a country with a high level of internal migration and broken marriages.

Once in São Paulo, the whole family lived in a single room behind a bar. They had to share the toilet with the customers. Later Lula recalled his embarrassment at inviting friends home from school because there was no chair for them to sit on. It was then, he says, that he realised for the first time that his family was poor. At 12, Lula got his first full-time job, working in a dry-cleaners. After being sacked he looked around for other odd jobs, working as a boot-black and then as an office-boy. He got these jobs in the informal labour market, with none of the benefits guaranteed in labour legislation.

At the age of 14, Lula got his first registered job, working in a warehouse. Later he found work in an engineering company and, as a result, managed to enrol on a three-year part-time course to train as a lathe operator. During this period he had an accident during a night shift. He was replacing a nut on a machine while a colleague held down the brake, but his colleague nodded off. The blade slipped forward, cutting off Lula's little finger on his left hand; he was 18 years old at the time. Apart from work, his main interests were girls and football. He was a keen supporter of the Corinthians football club in São Paulo.

In 1966 Lula started work at Villares, one of the biggest engineering firms in the country. In May 1969 he married Maria de Lourdes, a young worker in a textile factory. The following year Maria died attempted to give birth to their still-born child. She had been suffering from hepatitis, but it had not been diagnosed by the doctors. In 1973 Lula had a brief relationship with a young nurse, Miriam Cordeiro. They had a daughter and called her Luriam, following the practice common among the Brazilian working class of inventing a new name by combining the father's name with the mother's. The following year Lula married Marisa Letícia, a widow with one son. Marisa and Lula had three children, all boys.

Until this point there had been nothing to distinguish Lula's life from that of thousands of other migrants from the north-east with similar tales of hunger, suffering and limited social advancement despite years of effort. But Lula then shot to national prominence as the leader of the massive wave of strikes that swept through São Paulo's industries in 1978 and 1979 and a founder of what has become Latin America's most important left-wing political party. In telling the story, we shall as far as possible use Lula's own words and those of his colleagues in testimonies recorded by several authors, particularly the Chilean socialist Marta Harnecker in her excellent book, *O Sonho era Possível*. Other sources include *Without Fear of Being Happy* by Emir Sader and Ken Silverstein and *Lula, O Metalúrgico: Anatomia de uma Liderança* by Marco Morel.

* * *

According to Lula, his first contact with the union movement came through his brother, José Ferreira da Silva, known as Friar Chico because of his monk-like haircut. As a member of the banned Brazilian Communist Party, Lula's brother was active in underground politics. In 1969 he asked Lula, then working at an engineering plant in São Bernardo, an industrial town on the outskirts of São Paulo, to stand on his slate in the elections for the leadership of the metalworkers' union of São Bernardo and Diadema. Lula recalls: 'I was a lathe operator, I was earning reasonably well and I had a girlfriend. I wanted to play football, I wanted to go out dancing, I didn't want to know about union matters.'

But Lula reluctantly agreed to stand and, once elected, gradually became more involved in the union, but never followed his brother into the Communist Party. Though he refused to define himself ideologically, he became firmly opposed to the existing union leadership, which at that time was in the hands of *pelegos*, conservative union leaders who worked closely with the employers (see p. 52, note 6). Then, strangely enough, in 1975 Paulo Vidal, one of the old guard, asked Lula to stand in the upcoming election for union president. With hindsight, Lula believes he was being used in an internal power struggle.

> I had never spoken at a union assembly, had never used a microphone, so – and this is a supposition – when Paulo nominated me, I think he was planning to prove – not just to the leadership, but to all the workers as well – that he was irreplaceable and that I was a shit and couldn't get a damn thing done.

If this was Paulo Vidal's hidden agenda, his plan backfired. Lula was elected with 92 per cent of the vote and turned out to be an efficient and highly effective union leader.

A turning point for Lula came later that same year. His brother, Friar Chico, was arrested and charged with being a Communist 'subversive'. Lula learnt of his brother's arrest during a brief stopover in the United States on his way back from a conference in Japan, his first trip abroad. When a lawyer advised Lula to stay in the USA for a while, until the situation cooled down, Lula is reported to have replied:

> Look my friend, I don't speak the language of the people here, I've got no money, the food stinks, there's no rice, no beans. I'd rather be arrested in Brazil than stay in this dump of a country.

According to Lula, the arrest was

> the main reason why I lost all my inhibitions. Before, I had been a typical union leader. I had been afraid of being arrested. I had been worried about my family. I had never thought that being a union activist required very much. But, after my brother was arrested, I lost my fear.

But several other activists, particularly one of the big names in Brazilian theatre at the time, Lélia Abramo, say that this account is somewhat simplistic. As will be discussed later in this chapter, Lélia Abramo believes that, while Lula may have changed his ideas about what was demanded of a union leader at this time, it took longer for him to gain the courage to stand up to the authorities who had ruled Brazil for so long without being seriously challenged.

Buoyed up by his own militancy, Lula sought to change the way unions operated, improvising as he went along. When he took over, unions were largely apolitical. Workers turned to them for subsidised health treatment and other social benefits, not for real support in their demands for higher wages or better working conditions. The unions only came to life during the annual wage negotiations, and even then the wage increase was often worked out behind closed doors, with little more than symbolic participation from the workers themselves. In keeping with the government's wage policy at the time, there was no direct bargaining between unions and employers; wage increases were set by the government for the whole industry. Lula and the other young union leaders working with him decided that all this must change, but they began by making what seemed to be small adjustments:

> Our first big decision was not just to wait for workers to come to union assemblies at the time of our annual wage increase, but for us to seek them out at the factory gates and get them involved in other issues. We knew we had to get the workers to have more trust in us. So do you know what I did? I started to arrange football championships: the union leadership against factory teams. Before the matches began, I used to talk to the workers for five minutes. After the game we had a few beers and cooked a barbecue.

The union leaders also tried to make the issues more accessible.

I noticed that workers used to throw away the bulletin we gave them at the factory gates, when they were 50 yards or so down the road. I realised that they were chucking it away because it had nothing in it that interested them. So we decided to liven it up, to introduce cartoons, to turn it into an attractive four-page leaflet. The result: the workers didn't throw it away but put it in their pocket to read inside the factory.

In a short time, we managed to create a new awareness. Before, the union building had always been empty, no one took part in anything, but soon all our assemblies were crowded. What was the great advantage in doing this? It was to make the worker feel that the union belonged to him, was a body that would fight for him, go on the offensive for him. For instance, we started doing something that the workers loved – we printed in our journal the names of the line managers who treated them unfairly. In all, I think we achieved in three years things that normally in this country would have taken thirty.

From the beginning, Lula insisted on his own approach. Another union leader, Paulo Skromov, recalls:

Lula had an interesting, if disconcerting, way of doing things. For example, when he was re-elected president of the union, I think it was in January 1978 – I remember Lula was still very thin, and wore flares – he invited the São Paulo state governor and the Commander of the Second Army to the ceremony. For us, trade unionists on the left, this was completely nuts, this idea of inviting such authorities. He managed to upset both the right and the left.

In this unconventional way, Lula and the other leaders developed a union movement that in 1978 was able to mount the first serious challenge to the military government. Rejecting the wage rise offered by the government, the metalworkers opted for industrial action. The strike erupted in the Saab-Scania truck company in São Bernardo, spreading rapidly to other multinational companies such as Ford, Mercedes-Benz, Volkswagen and Chrysler. By the end of the second week, about 80,000 workers were on strike. 'It was the first major strike since 1968 and it received enormous support from all over the country' Lula remembers. 'In its way our 1978 strike meant for Brazilians what the Gdansk strike meant for the Poles. It was the first time since 1964 that Brazilian working class had shown such strength.'

More than the other strike leaders, Lula was determined not to allow left-wing intellectuals to rush in and take control of the strike movement. He stopped students from joining the pickets outside the factory gates, saying that they shouldn't get directly involved in a workers' struggle. It took a long while for him to begin to trust middle-class activists – even in the 1980s Lula could be heard reciting a phrase made famous by a samba school in Rio, 'It's intellectuals who love poverty. What the poor like is luxury.'

The left-wing actress, Lélia Abramo, remembers what it was like:

> I wanted to get involved in the strike movement so I went to São Bernardo to see Lula, but he refused to talk to me. He had something against artists, students and intellectuals. But the others – Djalma Bom, Devanir and Jac Bittar – they didn't feel the same way. In the end I managed to be quite useful. As I had been in Europe during the war, I knew how to distribute food parcels. I showed Devanir how to weigh out the rice in 1kg, 2kg bags and so on. He was very grateful. And in this way I got to know Lula. He finally started to talk to me and we became close friends.

The 1978 strike took the government and the car manufacturers completely by surprise. By the end of May, the union had a won a 24.5 per cent pay rise from the manufacturers, much more than they had originally offered. But according to Lula the wage increase was not the strike's main achievement:

> The great victory, even more than the wage rise itself, was that we forced the companies to negotiate an agreement directly with the union, without government interference.

Other strikes soon erupted in a number of industries around

the country. By the end of the year, over half a million workers were on strike and many won pay rises above those authorised by the government. The government's wage policy had come under serious threat for the first time.

Profile: Benedita da Silva

Benedita da Silva, Brazil's first black senator, remembers as a child delivering laundry to the house of President Juscelino Kubitschek in Leme in Rio de Janeiro. Her mother, a washer-woman, was a *mãe-de-santo*, a priestess in the Afro-Brazilian candomblé religion. 'At that time, it wasn't respectable for public figures to be seen consulting a *mãe-de-santo*', recalls Benedita, 'so they came secretly at night.' Benedita, one of 13 children, spent her childhood in a shanty-town built on stilts in a flooded area of Rio de Janeiro. The family was poor and from the age of six Benedita worked, first in street markets and then as a maid. 'Then I got a job in a smart nursery. I cleaned the bottoms of several leading public figures, whom I now meet as an equal', she laughs.

Benedita married at 15, just after her mother's death. By the time she was 22, she had five children. Her first husband, a house painter, was a heavy drinker. Even so, she stayed with him until his death 22 years later. Life was hard. In 1968 she could no longer earn enough to support herself and her children. 'I belong to the poorest of the poor in Brazilian society', she said. 'I'm one of the da Silvas of this life.' [In Brazil, da Silva is the commonest working-class surname.] She felt suicidal until a friend took her to one of the evangelical churches, the Assembly of God. It got her over this difficult period and she has been a devoted follower ever since, even giving up Carnival which she used to enjoy enormously.

'After the Bible, the PT', says Benedita. She was a founder member of the party and has been enormously active. Throughout her political career, she has turned the triple discrimination that she suffers into an electoral asset, using as her slogan, 'I am black, a woman and a shanty-town dweller'. She was a municipal councillor, then a federal deputy, becoming particularly active in the

Constituent Assembly, which in 1987 drew up Brazil's new constitution. She presented 92 amendments, 25 of which were approved, including the controversial measure to make the job of maid a proper, regulated profession. In 1994 Benedita was elected senator, a position she gave up in 1998 to become vice-governor of Rio de Janeiro in a coalition government. In early 2002 she became governor for the remaining nine months of the administration, as the outgoing governor, Anthony Garotinho, decided to stand for the presidency.

Benedita is a vehement defender of Brazil's black population. 'The Brazilian nation was forged through the rape of the black population', she says. 'Black families were destroyed. My ancestors were slaves. They had children who were taken away from them and sold. We have no idea what happened to them.' Until she became a well-known politician, Benedita used to suffer from discrimination. 'I used to go to the front entrance of apartment blocks and the porters would tell me to go round to the tradesmen's entrance.'

Benedita married again in 1982. Her second husband was a north-easterner with a long history of political involvement. In their heated political discussions, he cited Marx and Benedita replied with quotations from the Bible. He died in 1988 and Benedita married again, this time to the famous actor, Antônio Pitanga. Benedita waxes lyrical, 'I love my husband. I'm over the moon, passion 24 hours a day.'

Benedita still lives in the Chapéu Mangueira shanty-town where she has brought up her children. Like most shanty-towns in Rio, it is located on a hillside, forcing visitors to climb up 56 steep steps to get to Benedita's house. Though her three-roomed house is much more comfortable than most of the others, she still suffers from periodic police 'invasions', water shortages and electricity blackouts. Some years ago one of her nephews was killed in a shoot-out. After being elected senator, Benedita justified her decision to stay in the shanty-town by saying, *Sou favelada, estou senadora*, using the two verbs in Portuguese for 'to be', to say that her condition of life was to be a shanty-town dweller, whereas she was only temporarily a senator. She has become Minister of Social Assistance and Promotion.

By the following year, however, the government was better prepared and the unions faced a more difficult struggle. The metalworkers' union in São Bernardo called a general strike for 13 March, demanding a pay increase and improved working conditions. The response was overwhelming. The general assemblies, called by the union, had to be held in the Vila Euclides football stadium, the only place capable of holding more than 80,000 people. Lula describes the first assembly:

When we [the union leaders] arrived, the fences, the stadium, the grass, everywhere was full of people, and the podium was only a little table. The sound system wasn't even big enough for a small room, and I was alone, like a clown, on top of the table. Everyone was getting tense, and the leaders were beginning to argue, because the sound system wasn't any good and who knows what else was wrong.... You know what we did? We kept them there for four hours on the field without a sound system.... I yelled, the people in front of me repeated what I'd said and it was passed backwards.... When it started to rain, a few people started to leave. I shouted that no one there would dissolve in the rain and nobody else went away.

The strike was soon declared illegal, but Lula, showing a new willingness to take on the authorities, told a union assembly, 'They can declare the strike illegal, but it is just and legitimate, because its illegality is based on laws that weren't made by us and our representatives.' The experience was important for all the new union leaders, as Lula recalls:

I think that the first big lesson for us was that not one of us, individually, believed that we could do what we did. None of us believed that every blessed day, come sun come rain, we could get 80,000 workers into a football stadium. And when we were gathered there, all together, we realised that if we pooled our courage, together we became a giant. Individually, we all had qualms. We thought, 'we can't do this, we can't do that'. But together we did things that individually we thought impossible.

The union leaders were exhilarated by the political forces they had awakened. Paulo Skromov:

> It's something that happens rarely in history – that a mass-based movement erupts on the world stage at precisely the right moment, when there are sensitive leaders to take charge of it. At that time we weren't deluding ourselves when we said that we were going to transform the country, that we were creating a force that could free us from exploitation, from oppression. We were doing something of extreme importance. We were making history. There is nothing more exciting, more stimulating for mankind than to dream, and to believe that you can transform that dream into reality.

It was during the strike that Lula discovered his formidable talent for public speaking. Lula, who had never been very keen on reading books, had his own way of preparing his speeches, according to Paulo Skromov:

> Lula is someone who knows how to listen. He used to extract the best things from what he heard and make notes on his hand. He prepared his speeches with five, six or seven notes scribbled on the back of his hand.... Lula's speeches captivated people. They were rich in content and extraordinarily rich in form. People listened to him for half an hour and thought he had been speaking for two minutes at most. They wanted more. I remember very well how people looked when they were listening to him. They looked as if they were drinking it all in, savouring every drop.

But there were also difficult moments. 'During the 1979 strike, our union was taken over by the police for 15 days', said Lula. 'It was the first confrontation we had ever had with armed police, police dogs, firemen.'

There was also a time when Lula disappeared from view. The human rights lawyer, Luis Eduardo Greenhalgh, who was deeply involved in the new union movement from the early days, recalls, 'The Commander of the Second Army phoned Lula and threatened him, "You go to the assemblies and you'll be arrested". Lula, who had never had any contact with the army's brutal counter-insurgency units, ended up staying away from the assemblies.'

The other union leaders tried to make up for Lula's absence, recalls Paulo Skromov:

> Djalma Bom – he was the number two in the union – tried to take over Lula's role. But he didn't have the same impact as Lula, he didn't have his charisma. Though the workers trusted all the leaders, they wanted Lula. He had this incredible gift, something very personal. After two days like this, holding assemblies that attracted fewer and fewer people, we realised that the strike was losing momentum.

Several union leaders, together with Lélia Abramo, found out where Lula was hiding and went there. Paulo Skromov: 'We went into the house and found him, dressed in shorts, playing with his children on the carpet in the living room.'

Lélia Abramo takes up the story:

> David de Moraes said, 'We've come here to find out what's happened. It would be a good idea for you to go to the next assembly.' David's understated words would have been enough to persuade most people, but Lula didn't react. He stayed sitting on the floor, without saying anything. Then I asked if any other union leader wanted to speak. No one did. I'm telling you this not to talk about myself, but to tell you how it happened. So I said: 'Look, Lula, I didn't come here to praise you or to complain about you. I came here to tell you that you are coming with me to the assembly. I'm going to take you there.'

Perhaps because she was a woman, Lélia Abramo was able to say things that Lula wouldn't have accepted from any of the men present. According to Paulo Skromov:

> Lélia was wonderful, incredible. We didn't know what to say to Lula, but he listened to her and then turned to us and said, 'You're right. I reckon I'm wrong. I'll come back with you.'

Lula adds:

I had been banned by the authorities. It wasn't easy to take over running the strike again. But when I realised that what I was doing was causing serious problems for the movement, I decided to go back, even if it meant putting my neck on the guillotine.

Lélia Abramo continues:

I took him back. We went into the large room. It was packed. There must have been about 2,000 people there. He walked around the room and then, when he reached the head table, he burst into tears, started to sob. He was cheered. It lasted for at least ten minutes. He recovered himself and made a wonderful speech. For the first time he aligned himself politically with the opposition. He had never done this before.

Even so, the strike was by no means an unqualified success. On 21 March, eight days after the strike began, the labour minister agreed to direct talks between the unions and their employers, but insisted first on an immediate return to work by the strikers. This was overwhelmingly rejected by the strikers, but after heavy intimidation by the military police, many people began to drift back to work. In an effort to limit the damage, Lula accepted the employers' proposal for a 45-day truce and a 15 per cent wage rise, in exchange for a promise not to carry out reprisal sackings of union militants.

Lula's handling of the negotiations was bitterly criticised by many workers and some of his fellow union leaders. He was even jeered in the stadium when he explained his actions. Paulo Skromov:

We thought he had made a terrible mistake. Jacó began to cry. I tried to comfort him, but I was feeling much the same myself.

Lula:

Many workers left the stadium that night calling me a traitor, saying that I had sold them down the river, that I had betrayed them. It was a very difficult period for me. Political scientists said that I would never again be able to organise a strike, to regain the confidence of the workers. Paulo Skromov said that I was politically destroyed.

Paulo Skromov:

I was having lunch with Lula shortly afterwards, in the union canteen. A worker came up to our table and angrily threw down his union membership card in front of Lula. We looked at Lula. It was fairly tense. But Lula only lowered his head and the worker eventually walked off. Lula turned to us and said, 'That's nothing compared to other things I've had to go through since the end of the strike.

But some union leaders supported Lula. Wagner Benevides recalls:

Many workers thought that we could have continued, but it wasn't true. The strike had to stop. Everyone was exhausted. It had reached a critical moment. Lula took the only sensible decision, and his prestige suffered as a result. But Lula recovered. He was born again out of the ashes.

The 1979 strike convinced Lula and other union leaders of the need to create their own political party. They had received minimal support from Congress, even from those who claimed to be part of the opposition, which strengthened their distrust of professional politicians. The engineering companies subsequently reneged on their promise not to carry out reprisal sackings, further convincing the union leaders that they needed to take part directly in politics to fight for fairer laws on industrial action. A new phase in Brazilian history was about to begin.

Note

1   Quoted in Sue Branford and Bernardo Kucinski, *Carnival of the Oppressed – Lula and the Brazilian Workers' Party*, Latin America Bureau, London 1995, p. 34.

Profile: José Genoíno

Born into a poor rural family in the state of Ceará in the north-east, like millions of others Genoíno migrated to the south of the country in search of work. He became active in left-wing politics in the 1960s and was forced underground by the military, joining an ill-fated attempt by left-wing activists to flee into the Amazon forest to prepare for a rural guerrilla war. The few dozen activists were soon discovered and were crushed in a major army offensive involving 15,000 troops.

Genoíno was one of the few to survive. Badly tortured, he was eventually convicted by a military court. After serving his sentence, he was released and immediately got involved in politics once again. He was one of the founder members of the PT, and in November 1982 he was elected federal deputy for the PT on the most radical of platforms. He has remained in Congress ever since, becoming one of the PT's most important leaders.

Genoíno now belongs to the moderate, parliamentary faction of the PT. In 1990 he and Tarso Genro, another original thinker, who later became mayor of Porto Alegre, wrote a series of articles, published in the *Folha de S. Paulo*, in which they called for far-reaching changes to the party's reform programme. One of the articles demanded an end to what it called 'left-wing radicalism', which, the authors claimed, was inflicting a great deal of damage on the whole socialist project. When criticised by some PT factions for betraying his earlier ideals, Genoíno replied, 'If I want to reform the world, I have to accept the challenge of being reformed myself.'

In 1998 Genoíno was re-elected with a large majority for his fifth term as federal deputy. He became leader of the opposition in Congress and played an extremely important role in organising opposition to some of Fernando Henrique Cardoso's neo-liberal reforms.

Lula on the campaign trail

I spent the month of October 2002 filming Lula for a documentary that Eduardo Coutinho and I are making on Lula. I accompanied him to a dozen states and some 20 cities, besides Brasília. In all these places, Lula was welcomed by a huge crowd of people. Men, women, young, old, adolescents, they all went out on the streets in the name of something that we see rarely today – political enthusiasm.

The Lula phenomenon can only be properly understood by those who see him in the street. It isn't captured by the newspapers or by television. Or at least not fully. You have to be near him and see it for yourself. There are other events like this. The ones that occur to me immediately don't have anything to do with politics. Football and Carnival, for instance. Whoever has been to a football match at Maracanã or watched a samba school dance down the Marquês de Sapucaí [a street in Rio de Janeiro] and then sees the same event on television, knows that that the experience has been diminished. The same thing happens with great natural disasters (and, for those who have faith, religious ceremonies). These events all have to be experienced in the flesh, without mediation.

However, when people go to hear Lula, they expect more than the good time they get from going to a football match or watching a Carnival parade. Perhaps a few people went to some of the early rallies just to hear the singers, like Zezé di Camargo and Luciano, who were on the stage with Lula, but in the run-up to the final round of the elections, Lula went on the podium alone, often very late at night. He only arrived at Aracaju at 11 p.m., having been to three states earlier in the day. On the Wednesday before the election, in Florianópolis, Lula only began speaking just before mid-night, having been to all five regions of Brazil in that single day. Even so, the public squares were always crammed with people, not an inch of asphalt free.

In front of Lula were thousands of people who believed in him, in the possibility of changing Brazil, in the chance of improving their own lives. We don't know if they were right to have this faith in him. We'll only know that at the end of his government. What is undeniable is that Lula has exhumed the old idea of Utopia, bringing it back to the realm of political action.

Seeing Lula and his thousands of supporters flowing through the narrow streets of João Pessoa like a mighty river, I realised that what makes him different is not so much his proposals (there was little to choose between those of the four main candidates) but the open, sincere, unabashed conviction with which he defends his ideas. In that single day Lula spoke in Natal, Recife and Aracaju. Everywhere it was the same: the city coming to a standstill to hear a man proclaim his views with passion.

I hadn't seen anything like it for a long while. The last time was probably 20 years ago, during the big street campaigns for direct presidential elections. Since then things have changed a lot. Many of the brightest people in the centre and the left of the political spectrum have discarded the Utopian side of politics and become obsessed with technical expertise. The problem with expertise is that it is never charismatic. Expertise doesn't fill public squares; it doesn't spark off processions like the one I saw in João Pessoa. Expertise ignores an important side of life – call it the imagination, the spirit, the soul, whatever you like. It was always a mistake to suppose that people would be happy with technical expertise. They're not. If they just have that, their lives feel unfulfilled.

I think that when you offer people the chance to become part of a big project, of a shared dream, then they generally respond positively. This is Lula's great strength. He restores a sense of community. When he speaks, he seems to be offering everyone the chance of helping to make history. Lula probably never believed that Utopias were extinct. You just have to look at his life. No one has more authority than Lula to say that you can create your own history. When thousands of people went out onto the streets in Osasco (25 September), Porto Alegre (30 September and 18 October), Aracaju (15 October), João Pessoa (15 October), Recife (15 October), Belém (23 October), Macapá (23 October) and Florianópolis (30 September and 23 October), they did it not just because they wanted to see a politician (even though he is probably the best mass politician since Getúlio Vargas) but because they wanted to believe in the metaphor. Lula is proof that Brazil can be different.

With Lula the left has recovered the right to dream. But, unlike the right in Europe (and to a lesser extent in the United States), his dream is not founded on the idea of oppposition (to immigrants, Muslims, minorities in general) but of inclusion (of the poor, the marginalised). It is a generous Utopia.

But why did Lula manage to convince the country in 2002 and not in 1989, 1994 and 1998? In those years of defeat, the intensity of his belief was as strong as it is today. Apart from the well-known reasons – Collor's false promises, the apparently invincible *Plan Real*, the fear of economic instability, and now the wish for a change in direction – it seems that Lula's less aggressive tone played a part. Radical discourse only impassions those at the extremes, or near them. Today Lula manages to include almost everyone in his dream, even those who earlier felt rejected by his radical rhetoric.

Whether his Utopia can be achieved is another question. Lula believes sincerely that it can, and this turns him into that rarest of mortals: a politician that talks to the crowds from a soapbox without being a populist. Lula doesn't promise anything that he knows he cannot deliver. He doesn't encourage Messianism. And that's another positive aspect of his rallies: you have the feeling that the peole there aren't handing over their lives to a charismatic leader to resolve everything for them. Even the rhetoric Lula uses is cautious and reticent. When all that is needed is a final rhetorical flourish for a certain train of thought to set the crowd alight, Lula deliberately lowers the volume of his voice, changes the stress of the sentence, brings the crowd back to earth, with a gentle landing. It is a way of respecting the crowd and of resisting the easy temptation to hold it in his spell.

Lula won this election believing passionately in his ideas. But this isn't enough to govern well. If technical expertise without Utopia is as arid as a desert, Utopia without efficiency is like a bout of heavy drinking – wonderful at the time but dreadful afterwards. We must hope that Lula can pull off the difficult synthesis of combining the two.

Few have managed it. Despite all the criticisms that have been made of Juscelino Kubitschek [President of Brazil in 1956–60] – the delirious dream of Brasília, the development model that concentrated income, the beginning of the inflationary spiral – he was perhaps the last leader to have had some success in this task. For a few years Brazil seemed to pull it off. We grew a lot, we invented new things, we gained in self-esteem. The people were happy. It's a long while ago. We want to have that feeling again.

João Moreira Salles

Lula – no right to fail

'When I arrived, several men and women came up to me, crying and saying that I am their last hope. I know that I cannot fail. I know that I cannot betray the dreams of the millions and millions of Brazilians who are backing me. Any other President of the Republic can be elected and not do anything. The Brazilian people are used to this. But I don't have that right, for there are people out there in the crowd who have been supporting me for 10, 20, 30 years.

We can't perform miracles. The country is engulfed in an unprecedented crisis. The economy hasn't been growing for eight years. I don't know if I can achieve everything I want to, but you can be sure that I'm going to start doing what is necessary, then what is possible, and finally doing the impossible.

They said that Lula can't be a candidate because he doesn't speak English, he doesn't speak French, he doesn't have a university degree, he still has a mark on his hand from when he was injured as an industrial worker. I want to tell you, with pride, that I don't want to forget my origins. I want to prove that a metalworker is capable of governing this country better than the Brazilian elite has managed over the last hundred years or so, since the Republic was created.'

(Lula speaking at a rally in Fortaleza on 23 October 2002)

3
The Fernando Henrique Cardoso Legacy

SUE BRANFORD

On election night on 27 October 2002, Lula was interviewed on *Jornal Nacional*, the main news and current affairs programme on TV Globo, the country's leading television network. The programme had carried in considerable detail the reaction of the so-called 'market' to Lula's victory – the small slide in the value of the *real* on the currency market, the impact on the São Paulo stock market, the view of foreign investors. With a half smile on his face, Lula commented ironically: 'Haven't we got something more important to talk about? What about the hunger, the unemployment and the social injustice in the country?' With this observation, Lula was saying indirectly that he intends to change priorities and to place Brazil's social crisis at the heart of policy making. It is for this reason that his victory could become a turning point in Latin American history, for it is the first time for 30 years that a President, backed by a large and solid political party, has been elected on the back of programme that is questioning the central tenet of neo-liberalism, namely that the most important role of government is to create favourable conditions for private investors. But how easy will it be for the PT to make this shift in priorities? What kind of legacy has Cardoso left after his eight years in government?

The Cardoso years

When Fernando Henrique Cardoso took office on 1 January

1995, he stood for the best of the old elitist civilian governments that had ruled Brazil for much of the twentieth century (outside the period of the 1964–85 military dictatorship): he was a respected intellectual, he spoke four or five languages, he was a democrat who opposed the military dictatorship, and he was personally honest. Moreover, before entering politics, Cardoso had established an international reputation as a left-leaning sociologist who had studied 'dependent development' in Latin America, and had concluded that, far from bringing autonomous development, the close relationship that the region had developed with the rich, industrialised countries, particularly the United States, had exacerbated social and economic inequalities and increased vulnerability to external shocks. He had argued that Latin America's spineless and cowed 'national bourgeoisie' was incapable of using an alliance with 'external monopoly capital' to defend its own interests[1] and concluded that the region must forge its own identity and independent path to development.

Because his ideas were considered 'subversive' by the military government, Cardoso was forced into exile in the late 1960s. When he returned in 1978, he decided to enter politics and in 1980 he was one of the founders of the Partido do Movimento Democrático Brasileiro (PMDB), the main opposition party at the time. Having been elected senator in 1982, winning more votes than any other candidate, he helped to restore civilian government in 1985 and learnt how to operate effectively within the corrupt, clientelistic world of Brazilian politics. By the time he was elected President in 1994, it was evident that he had abandoned most of his radical views: in his desire to defeat Lula and the PT, he formed an alliance with the Liberal Front Party, the stronghold of reactionary landowners and old-style political bosses. Cardoso even said, in front of television cameras, 'Forget everything I have ever written.'

Even so, few people expected Cardoso to become a convert to the latest – and particularly vicious – variant of 'dependent development'. By the time Cardoso ended his eight years in government, international capital had taken over huge areas of the Brazilian economy and the country was caught in a foreign debt trap of unprecedented proportions. Unemployment – and crime – had reached record levels. One analyst concluded: 'The Brazilian case constitutes a laboratory experiment demonstrating how and why the injection of the neo-liberal virus, especially that strain which includes a pegged exchange rate, tends to polarise society and ruin an economy.'[2]

The *Plano Real*

By 1990 Cardoso had been completely converted to neo-liberalism and would have accepted a ministry in the Collor de Melo government, the first administration to apply free market reforms, if he had not been stopped by his politically astute colleague, Mário Covas. After Collor was forced to resign after a huge corruption scandal, Cardoso agreed to become finance minister in the government set up by his successor, Itamar Franco. In early 1994 he announced a radically different kind of anti-inflationary plan, called the *Plano Real*, which was implemented piecemeal and culminated on 1 July 1994, amid much fanfare, with the introduction of a solid new currency, the *real*, anchored to the US dollar. The plan succeeded in very rapidly bringing down inflation to manageable levels. For several years, runaway inflation had been the scourge of the country, reaching 1,158 per cent in 1992 and 2,709 per cent in 1993. While the massive price increases had wreaked havoc on all Brazilian lives, they had particularly affected the poor, who were paid in cash and, unlike the middle classes, did not have the protection of index-linked bank accounts. Before converting the price of retail goods to the new currency in the last stage of the plan, the government increased the minimum wage, which is the yardstick for all payments, including pensions, made to the poorer classes. So, as well as benefiting from the end of inflation, the poor received a real income boost.

With inflation down to manageable levels, it became possible once again to pay for goods in instalments in the department stores, and the poor went on a spending spree, buying basic household goods, such as televisions and washing machines, which they had not been able to afford during the years of high inflation. The economy, which after several years of stagnation had already grown by 4.9 per cent in 1993, as foreign capital began to enter the economy as a result of the early round of free market reforms, expanded by a further 5.9 per cent in 1994, as poorer Brazilians joined in the party. The whole country breathed a collective sigh of relief, as the nightmare years receded and the population recovered its faith in the future. The PT was caught off balance by the success of the plan, which they did not know whether to praise or condemn. The main beneficiary was Cardoso, widely regarded as the 'saviour of the nation', and with the backing of the right-wing Liberal Front Party he became the presidential candidate of the ruling party for the elections in October 1994. He won with a comfortable majority in the first round, while Lula suffered his second defeat, not even obtaining enough votes to force a second round.

While it is true that inflation had become so ingrained in Brazilian society that it took some kind of shock treatment to break its hold over society, it is also clear that the technocrats who backed the *Plano Real*, particularly the team that came into power with finance minister Pedro Malan on 1 January 1995 at the beginning of the Cardoso government, used the prestige they had gained from the plan as a means of implementing a fully-fledged neo-liberal programme, which they believed would finally launch Brazil on the road to full economic development. According to Luiz Carlos Bresser-Pereira, a leading Brazilian economist who was Minister of Federal Administration and State Reform during the first Cardoso administration (1995–8), the team had accepted uncritically the US-sponsored economic doctrine known as the Washington Consensus. Bresser-Pereira sums up the new orthodoxy in the following way:

> The recipe is simple: if a country completes its fiscal adjustment, if it carries out other neo-liberal reforms, and if it opens up the financial sector to the world market, then it will be rewarded by a big influx of foreign capital. Instead of the 'development-with-debt' that characterised the 1970s, it will have 'development-with-foreign savings'.[3]

According to Geisa Maria Rocha, a Brazilian economist who teaches political economy at Rutgers University in the USA, the Washington Consensus was sold to Brazil (among other developing countries) as the answer to all its problems: it was told that 'foreign direct investment would perform multiple services to the country: it would help finance balance-of-payments deficits, modernise industrial structures, develop advanced technology, promote productivity and promote the international competitiveness of Brazilians exports'.[4] Bresser-Pereira says that the Consensus was rapidly adopted by most developing countries because it seemed to incur no costs, only benefits.

The most fervent advocate of the Washington Consensus in the Cardoso government was Gustavo Franco, whose familiarity with US economic theory included a doctorate at Harvard University; he became first Director of International Affairs and then president at the Central Bank. One commentator said that: 'Cardoso considered Franco's ideas as a kind of Copernican Revolution',[5] that is, he believed that they made possible an entirely new – and self-evidently superior – way of viewing the world of international finance. In a newspaper interview in October 1996, Cardoso commented:

> We have achieved something that neither Marx nor Weber nor anyone else imagined – they couldn't have done at the time they lived. Capital has internationalised rapidly and is available in

abundance. Some countries can take advantage of this excess of capital, and Brazil is one of them.[6]

Totally won over to the new ideology, Cardoso did not spare his critics, calling them 'catastrophists' and 'doom-mongers'; he even invented a new term – *neobobo* (neofool) – for those Luddites who criticised the neo-liberals and refused to recognise the wonderful opportunities opened up by the globalised world.

In line with neo-liberal thinking, the Cardoso government took measures to change the role of the state, cutting back on public spending and privatising many large state companies, including some that were perfectly sound. As controlling inflation was seen as an essential part of the programme, it also kept the local currency at a high value with respect to the dollar, so that imports would remain cheap, and was delighted when in 1998 inflation was brought down to 1.7 per cent, a lower rate than in many industrialised countries. The high value of the *real* meant that Brazilian goods became expensive abroad, so Brazil began to run a trade deficit (see Table 3.1) but, as there was plenty of foreign capital coming into the country, this was not seen as a problem but as a means of acquiring foreign goods cheaply.

Not surprisingly, since they had been masterminded in the USA, Brazil's new policies were warmly welcomed abroad. The world economy was suffering from a huge glut of capital, with financial institutions in the rich countries desperately searching for new sources of short-term profit. The decision by many developing countries, under guidance from Washington, to open up new opportunities for speculative investment, particularly the hugely lucrative foreign exchange market, came as a godsend. According to the economist Harry Shutt,

> the global volume of business [in the foreign exchange market] rose over tenfold in constant value terms between the early 1980s and the mid-1990s – to a level estimated at no less than US$1,500

Table 3.1 Brazil's Balance of Payments (US $ billions)

	1993	1994	1995	1996	1997	1998	1999	2000	2001	2002	2003
a) Trade											
Exports	38.5	43.5	46.5	47.7	52.9	51.1	48.8	55.0	56.2	51.3*	54.7*
Imports	-25.2	-33.1	-49.8	-53.3	-61.3	-57.7	-49.2	-55.7	-55.5	-42.7*	-41.7*
Balance	13.3	10.4	-3.4	-5.5	-8.3	-6.5	-1.2	-0.6	2.6	8.6*	13.0*
b) Services											
Interest	-8.4	-6.3	-8.1	-9.8	-10.6	-11.9	-15.2	-15.0	-14.8	n.a.	n.a.
Profits and dividends	-1.9	-2.4	-2.5	-2.4	-5.5	-7.1	-4.0	-3.5	-4.9	n.a.	n.a.
Other	-3.5	-3.4	-3.9	-5.4	-6.3	-7.8	-5.0	-5.5	-6.1	n.a.	n.a.
Balance	-13.8	-12.1	-14.5	-17.6	-22.4	-26.9	-24.2	-24.0	-25.8	n.a.	n.a.
c) Current account	-0.5	-1.7	-17.9	-23.1	-30.7	-33.4	-25.4	-24.6	-23.2	-14.9*	-8.6*
Debt payments	-9.2	-11.0	-11.0	14.4	-28.7	-33.5	-49.5	-34.6	-35.2	n.a.	n.a.
Gross external debt	145.7	148.2	159.2	179.9	199.9	241.6	241.4	236.8	210.8**	n.a.	n.a.

*Economist Intelligence Unit predictions

** As of March 2001 and retroactive to 2000, the Central Bank adopted a new method of calculation of the external debt that reduced its stock by about US$30.1 billion.

Sources: Banco Central do Brasil, Geisa Maria Rocha, Economist Intelligence Unit and my calculations.

billion *a day* by 1995. Its attraction for investing institutions – particularly commercial banks – are obvious, since it involves dealing in the most liquid of all assets (cash), of which they are bound in any case to hold large quantities and which can be placed in interest-bearing deposits for very short periods.[7]

Awash with foreign capital

Foreign direct investment poured into Brazil, with the annual net total going from US$3.9 billion in 1995 to US$9.6 billion in 1996, US$17.8 billion in 1997, US$26.3 billion in 1998, US$29.9 billion in 1999 and US$30.5 billion in 2000.[8] According to the United Nations Commission on Trade and Development (UNCTAD), Brazil's stock (that is, the total amount) of foreign direct investment rose from US$42.5 billion (6 per cent of GDP) in 1995 to US$197.7 billion (21.6 per cent of GDP) in 1999.[9] Not surprisingly, Brazil was fêted around the globe as the latest 'wonder' of the developing world.

While many analysts, particularly on the left, believe that it is harmful for key sectors of the productive economy to be under foreign control, because multinationals do not consider national interests when taking investment decisions, orthodox economists have long argued that foreign direct investment is beneficial for a developing country, because it allows a country to have a higher rate of investment and thus to grow more rapidly. This argument makes the common-sense assumption that foreign capital does not replace national savings, but complements them. So did this happen? Did the big influx of foreign investment that Cardoso so strongly promoted lead to a higher rate of investment?

Rather surprisingly, Luiz Carlos Bresser-Pereira, who was actually a member of the government when these policies were being adopted, discovered that foreign investment had little impact on Brazil's overall rate of investment:

During the Fernando Henrique Cardoso government foreign direct investments increased extraordinarily: until 1994 the country received at most US$2 billion *a year* in foreign investments; after the *Plano Real* the country received on average US$2 billion *a month* in direct investments. But, contradicting conventional wisdom, the rate of capital formation did not increase and the growth in per capita income remained at around 1 per cent per capita.[10]

These figures strongly suggest that most of the inflows of foreign capital did not constitute investment in completely new fixed assets, which is what UNCTAD used to mean by foreign direct investment and which is generally seen as beneficial to the receiving economy. Other uses, it seems, were made of most of the money. Some of it went on the takeover of existing assets. Indeed, the Brazilian government was at this time encouraging such a trend through its huge privatisation programme in which state companies were sold to multinationals, often at knock-down prices. The government expected the multinationals to invest heavily in the companies they purchased, but in most cases this did not happen. So the Brazilian people got a raw deal: they handed over control of key sectors of the economy without getting the increase in productive investment (and the influx of sophisticated technology) that was supposed to be their recompense in the *quid pro quo*. Another part of the money appears to have gone to the lucrative local money market where, as will be discussed in more detail later, the government was paying exorbitantly high interest rates in its desperate need to raise the money to roll over the huge domestic and foreign debts.

Bresser-Pereira points to another complementary 'perverse mechanism' at the very heart of the Washington Consensus that added to the harm done by the big influx of foreign capital. It is a simple mechanism that stems not from decisions taken by individual companies, but from the nature of the macro-economic policy itself in a situation of almost complete trade liberalisation. It works as follows: a big influx of foreign capital means that foreign currency becomes more widely available, so the dollar depreciates against the local currency; this means that the purchasing power of wages, paid in local currency, increases vis-à-vis the dollar; this, in turn, leads both to an increase in consumption, particularly of imported goods, and to a concomitant decline in domestic savings by individuals; this shortfall in domestic savings is covered by foreign capital. The net result is an unchanged rate of capital formation but a worsening trade account, because of the surge in imports.

Bresser-Pereira concludes that, despite all the promises, Brazil along with the other countries taken in by the Washington Consensus gained very little at all from the influx of capital:

> The developing country absorbs foreign savings and acquires great foreign obligations, but it does not increase its capacity to remunerate the foreign investments. The new consensus thus served the interests of commercial and investment banks in the rich countries, which are constantly looking for new profitable outlets for their glut of capital. And it brought great benefits to the governments of the rich countries, as they are always keen to increase their trade surpluses. So it naturally received the support of the two international financial institutions based in Washington: the IMF and the World Bank.[11]

In Brazil's case, the impact on the trade account was dramatic: the country went from routine trade surpluses of around US$10 billion in the early 1990s to heavy deficits – US$3.4 billion in 1995, US$5.5 billion in 1996, US$8.3 billion in 1997 and US$6.5 billion in 1998. The deficit on the current account (that is, the balance left after trade in goods and services, income flows and current transfers have been taken into account, excluding capital movements) went up from US$1.7 billion in 1994, when Brazil still had a healthy trade balance, to US$17.9 billion in 1995, US$23.1 billion in 1996, US$30.7 billion in 1996 and US$33.4 billion in 1998 (see

Table 3.1). Throughout Brazil's history high current account deficits have usually been a sign that a crisis was approaching and this was to prove no exception.

The deficits led to a startling increase in the country's foreign vulnerability. Once again, it is easy to see what happened. Brazil needed a big influx of foreign capital (apart from foreign investment) to cover the current account deficits and to build up its foreign reserves to protect its overvalued currency from attacks by speculators. In order to attract this foreign capital, the government (which borrows in the local currency, the *real*, on the local money market) had to raise interest rates to one of the highest levels in the world and lay on other attractive enticements for foreigners (such as indexing treasury bonds against the US dollar and authorising investors to set up bank accounts with free access to floating exchange rates, so that they could move funds in and out of the country at will).[12] In its turn, the high rate of interest led to a ballooning internal debt, which by the end of the Cardoso government had reached over 50 per cent of GDP. The foreign debt, too, grew very quickly (just it had, in very different circumstances, in the late1970s), increasing from US$145.7 billion in 1993 to US$241.4 billion in 1999. Even discounting foreign reserves of around US$35 billion, this left a net debt of US$206 billion in 1999, which was more than four times that year's exports of US$44.8 billion. The IMF and the World Bank believe that in most cases a ratio of net foreign debt to exports of more than 2.5 leaves an economy extremely vulnerable to external shocks.

As Geisa Maria Rocha has shown, Brazil's susceptibility soon became evident during the Cardoso government. The country no sooner recovered from one shock than it was shaken by another: first, the collapse of the Mexican peso in 1995 and the subsequent aftershocks throughout Latin America; next, the East Asian crisis in early 1997; and then the Russian default in August 1998, followed by the plunge in Wall Street in the autumn. Each time the crisis took the same relentless course –

speculators withdrew their 'hot money', the government increased interest rates to super-high levels in a desperate attempt to attract the capital back, the Brazilian economy stalled as companies reeled from the high cost of borrowing, recession, and finally a modest recovery.

This chain of events, which has been repeated in so many vulnerable countries in the world over the last decade, does incalculable damage to the developing nation. Because the debtor country is so dependent on capital inflows, it is vulnerable to deliberate attacks, engineered by speculators to increase their takings. At these moments Brazil's 'country risk' – the sanctimonious and self-righteous term with which speculators justify their exorbitant takings by claiming that they must be rewarded for the high risk they are taking in lending to an untrustworthy country – rose to over 1,500 points (even going to the ludicrous level of 2,500 points at one stage in 2002). This meant that Brazil had to pay an additional rate of interest, above the US base rate, of 15 per cent (or even 25 per cent) a year. In practice, the banks have rarely paid the price of the additional risk they claim to be running, for whenever an important debtor has finally exhausted its reserves and faced default, the IMF has stepped in with extra cash, always demanding additional sacrifices from the recipient nation, even though almost all the new money has gone straightaway to the foreign banks.[13] This scheme has meant that for two decades the governments of debtor countries have been paying ludicrously high rates of interest and making big contributions to the exorbitant profits made by many foreign banks. This export of capital from the poorest to the richest nations – which dwarfs all assistance received by developing countries in aid – is one of the worst scandals of the present age.

For Brazil, the crisis was most serious in the first half of 1998, when US$31.2 billion in speculative capital haemorrhaged out of the country in a few weeks amid rumours that Brazil would follow Russia into default. Rather than let the *real* drop to its market level (which was bound to happen in the end, given the deregulated state of the Brazilian economy), the government spent half the country's foreign reserves in just two months in what was to prove a fruitless attempt to maintain the currency at its high level. Politics intervened when the USA organised an IMF bail-out worth US$41.5 billion to postpone the collapse of the currency until after Cardoso had been re-elected President in October (defeating Lula in his third attempt) but, after the election, market pressure on the *real* continued. According to Bresser-Pereira, a minister until the end of 1998, Finance Minister Pedro Malan refused to accept even then that his policy had failed: 'In January 1999, after a long internal struggle within the government, the President of the Republic, going against the advice of his Finance Minister, decided to let the exchange rate float.' If the government had insisted on keeping an overvalued currency until the last possible moment, as happened in neighbouring Argentina, Brazil's economic situation would undoubtedly be worse today. Surprisingly, Malan was not sacked, nor did he resign, after this major policy defeat (although the young Turk, Gustavo Franco, lost his job).

Because of the devaluation and the US government's decision to lower interest rates to prop up the US stock market, Brazil enjoyed a breather and the economy grew by 4.4 per cent in 2000. Yet before that year was out, the crisis returned in an even more virulent form. The flow of international capital, vital for covering the current account deficit, was halted by the looming default in Argentina and the downturn in the global economy, particularly in the United States. In August 2001 Brazil signed a new US$15 billion deal with the IMF, for which it was required to commit itself to a budget surplus of at least 3 per cent over the following three years. This time the respite was even shorter. After massive capital flight, Argentina ran out of money to service its US$150 billion foreign debt and, despite desperate efforts, was finally unable to protect its currency, the *peso*, which in January 2002 broke spectacularly out of the dollar straitjacket, falling from parity with the dollar to four *pesos* to the dollar in just a few weeks. Abandoned by the international financial community, Argentina sank into a deep depression, with output falling by about 15 per cent in 2002.

In 2002 rumours were rife that Brazil would soon be following Argentina down the road to total economic collapse (though this was never realistically on the cards, as Brazil's situation was quite different, particularly after the *real* had been devalued). In the middle of the year, with opinion polls suggesting that Lula would win the presidential election in October, speculators began to pull money out of the country, saying that they feared that Lula would repudiate the foreign debt and freeze the domestic debt. One bank – Goldman Sachs – even created a so-called 'Lula meter' in which it calculated the knock-on effect that the fluctuating predictions of a Lula victory had on the *real* in the currency market and on Brazil's foreign-debt rating in the financial market. In June, George Soros, the speculator-cum-philanthropist, told a Brazilian journalist in New York that Brazil faced economic meltdown if it elected Lula. He added: 'Brazil is condemned by the market to elect Serra [the government's candidate], for in global capitalism only Americans vote, not Brazilians.' The comment was seen in Brazil as outrageous interference in the country's internal democratic system and it probably helped to strengthen Lula's ratings in the opinion polls.

In August 2002 the international financial community, which had turned its back on Argentina, decided that a Brazilian default would be too disruptive for the already nervous world financial markets. The Bush administration, in particular, was keen to bail out First Boston and other US banks, large donors to the Republican Party, just before the mid-term elections. So the IMF agreed to another bail-out, of US$30 billion. In what was clearly intended as a manoeuvre to gain maximum political leverage for its loan, the IMF arranged for most of the money to be disbursed in February 2003, so that it could first get a commitment from the new President to agree to the IMF's conditions.

The social legacy

Just before Cardoso took office in January 1995, he told me in an interview for the BBC that he hoped to be remembered by posterity 'as the President who did most to resolve Brazil's serious social crisis'. Many Brazilians shared his hope, for their expectations had been aroused by the *Plano Real* which, as we have discussed, Cardoso introduced as Finance Minister during the Itamar Franco government. Because the plan put an end to runaway inflation and increased the minimum wage, it brought real benefits to the poor. In the following year (1995), the proportion of the population classified as 'poor' – that is, they do not spend enough money on food to cover their basic calorie requirements – fell by almost eight percentage points, to around 33 per cent of the population.[14]

The Cardoso government followed up this success by tackling some of the country's most pressing social problems, particularly in the area of public health. It set up an effective programme for dealing with HIV and AIDS, based on awareness building and the local production of generic drugs,[15] which means that this illness is now largely under control. It improved pre- and post-natal care, which led to a decrease in infant mortality from 48 deaths per thousand live births in 1994 to 35 deaths per thousand live births in 2000 (which is still quite high, with the rate fluctuating quite heavily between different regions and different social groups). It introduced some educational reforms, including the adoption in some parts of the country of the Bolsa-Escola scheme (by which the government provides a family with a basic income, provided the children attend school regularly). The rate of illiteracy fell from 19 per cent in 1991 to 13 per cent in 2000.

Table 3.2: Growth of Gross Domestic Product (GDP) across Three Decades

Period	GDP	Per capita GDP
1971–1980	8.63%	5.72%
1981–1990	1.57%	−0.37%
1991–2000	2.65%	1.11%

Source: Ipeadata – www.ipeadata.org.br

None of these achievements, however, could compensate for the impact on the country of the government's wholesale acceptance of neo-liberal policies, which meant that, after the initial gain under the *Plano Real*, no further progress was made in redistributing income from the rich to the poor. As Cardoso accepted the neo-liberal agenda that had dismantled worker rights and increased social inequalities all over the world, some social indicators (along with land concentration)[16] actually worsened during the Cardoso years. The government's only real chance of doing something effective for the poor would have been through strong economic growth, which could have brought some trickle-down benefits. But the specific characteristics of the Washington Consensus, with its strong emphasis on anti-inflationary policies, cutbacks in government spending and high interest rates, made this impossible: annual growth averaged just 2.6 per cent in the 1990s, which works out at an annual per capita rate of growth of just 1.1 per cent (see Table 3.2). It was only a small improvement on the rates achieved during the 'lost decade' of the 1980s, and it meant that the last period of sustained growth for Brazil was in the 1970s.

Sluggish economic growth meant that it became more and more difficult for a worker to find a proper registered job: according to official figures, which are known to underestimate the scale of the problem, unemployment increased from 4.5 million (6.1 per cent of the labour force) in December 1994 to

11.5 million (15 per cent of the labour force) in December 2000.[17] Unemployment was most prevalent among the young, with half of the unemployed being 25 years old or younger. More surprisingly perhaps, unemployment rates were higher for workers with four to seven years of schooling than for those with less then one year of schooling; this suggests that, far from helping Brazil to develop more sophisticated industrial sectors, which would increase the demand for skilled workers, neo-liberalism pushed Brazil back towards its old role as an undeveloped country whose main 'comparative advantage' on the world marketplace was its cheap, unskilled labour. Many of the unemployed tried to eke out a living in the informal market. By 2002 only one third (24 million) of Brazil's economically active population of 76.5 million people had a registered job, with some kind of labour rights. According to Sérgio Mendonça, director of DIEESE, the main trade union statistics department, 'the figures show that the informal market is more than saturated'.[18] Research shows that by 2002 workers in the informal sector in the city of São Paulo worked, on average, 76 hours a week and, even so, had an income of less than R$240 (about US$80) a month.

Even workers with proper, registered jobs felt the impact of the neo-liberal agenda, as the government came under pressure to 'flexibilise' the labour force. This was even written into one of the agreements with the IMF: item 33 of the 'memorandum of understanding' signed in 1998 stated: 'Though the labour market is not characterised by serious rigidities, determined regulations and labour market policies could contribute to a greater flexibility'.[19] However, the government's efforts to water down the labour safeguards written into both the progressive 1988 Constitution and the main body of the country's labour legislation met with fierce resistance from the labour unions. So Cardoso changed tactics: he opted for piecemeal changes, often introduced through the use of his special presidential powers. Among other initiatives, he created the much-hated 'temporary contract' (a kind of short-term contract under which workers are not given standard labour rights), he abolished the constitutional requirement that no worker should work more than 44 hours without receiving overtime payments, and he decided that Brazil should no longer adhere to Convention 158 of the International Labour Organisation (ILO) that places restraints on 'unmotivated dismissal'.

Not surprisingly, the combination of high unemployment and deteriorating labour conditions led to a fall in earnings: once inflation is taken into account, the average wage fell by 10.8 per cent from the end of 1997 to the end of 2001, even though Brazilian productivity was increasing during this period.[20] By 2001 Brazil had 57 million 'poor' people, of whom 25 million – that is, 15 per cent of the total population – were classified as 'indigent', that is, a subcategory within the 'poor' of people who do not have a large enough income to cover their basic calorie requirement, even if they spend all of it on food. Possibly because of the rise in unemployment, crime increased: more than 1,700 youngsters aged between 15 and 25 were assassinated in 2000, making Brazil one of the most violent countries in the world. Some of the international comparisons are surprising: from January 1998 to December 2001 467 children and youngsters met violent deaths in Israel and Palestine as a result of the conflict; during the same period 3,937 children and youngsters were shot dead in the city of Rio de Janeiro.[21]

So Brazil remains one of the most unjust countries in the world: the richest 1 per cent of the population, who amount to about 1.7 million people, divide between them 13.3 per cent of national income, a larger share of the cake than goes to the whole of the poorest half of the population, totalling 85 million people. As has been happening in many countries in the world, income distribution has actually been getting worse in Brazil, as the poorest 20 per cent received a significantly larger share of national income in 1960 than they did thirty years later (see

Table 3.3: Brazil's Income Distribution among the Economically Active Population

	1960	1979*	1990	1995	1999
Poorest 20%	3.5%	1.9%	2.1%	2.3%	2.3%
Poorest 50%	17.7%	11.9%	11.3%	12.3%	12.6%
Richest 20%	54.3%	64.2%	65.6%	64.2%	63.8%
Richest 10%	39.6%	47.6%	49.1%	47.9%	47.4%
Richest 1%	11.9%	13.4%	14.2%	13.9%	13.3%

Source: PNAD

* PNAD did not carry out a survey in 1980.

Table 3.3). This is largely because those with by far the biggest incomes throughout the world today are a relatively small group of speculators, who obtain most of their money not from their large salaries but from hugely lucrative deals on the global money markets. As a result, the share of national income going to wages has declined in many countries throughout the world: in Brazil it fell from 44 per cent of gross domestic product in 1993 to 36 per cent by 2000.[22] Extraordinary as it may appear, someone belonging to the rich elite – that is, the 1 per cent of extemely wealthy Brazilians – has an income 1,825 times greater than those belonging to the poorest 10 per cent of the population. Latin America is renowned throughout the world for its social inequality and, according to the United Nations Economic Commission for Latin America and the Caribbean (ECLAC), Brazil is the worst of the lot: it is the only country in the region in which income is so concentrated that more than half of the population earns less than half the average wage.[23]

Prospects

Shortly after his electoral victory, Lula started organising a Social and Economic Development Council with representatives from many different social groups, as the first step in mobilising the whole country in a national crusade to end social exclusion and to lay the foundations for a long period of economic growth and social prosperity. He also began to set up the party's flagship programme, entitled *Fome Zero* (Zero Hunger), which aims over three years to lift out of abject poverty the 9.3 million families (44 million people) that have a per capita income of less than one dollar a day, which is the benchmark set by the World Bank for calculating the breadline.

While the programme plans in the short term to issue food coupons, rather like the Food Stamps issued by the Roosevelt government during the Great Depression in the USA in the 1930s, the PT is aware that in the longer term it must break the vicious circle that currently produces thousands of new 'indigents' each year:

> The definitive resolution of the problem of hunger in Brazil demands a new model of economic development that promotes growth with income distribution, in order to increase the domestic market with the generation of more jobs, higher wages and, more precisely, a recovery in the purchasing power of the minimum wage, which acts as a kind of 'beacon' for the incomes of the poorer sectors of the population. In other words, to guarantee food security for the whole Brazilian population it is necessary to change the present economic model that creates social exclusion, of which hunger is just one of the visible results, along with unemployment, extreme poverty, and land and income concentration.[24]

Despite the ambitious scope of *Fome Zero*, the PT made it clear that the project was to be funded out of existing resources or new funds coming from abroad. Indeed, international financial institutions, including the World Bank, were rushing to offer funding (which the new government seemed prepared to accept, even though it would increase yet further the foreign debt and funding in dollars was particularly inappropriate for a programme that would be purchasing domestic products for domestic distribution). Even the powerful biotechnology lobby, headed by Monsanto, was proposing generous aid, in return for a commitment from the PT government to lift the ban on genetically modified crops; this was an offer that the PT seemed likely to decline. Other initiatives, such as Green Exchange, by which Brazil hopes to arrange food barter deals within the regional Mercosul trade pact (involving Brazil, Argentina, Paraguay and Uruguay), were imaginative and affordable.

Although nearly everyone in the party has welcomed *Fome Zero*, it falls short of the radical restructuring of society, promised by the PT since its foundation, that many *petistas* had hoped would lie at the heart of the new government's macro-economic policy. Despite some encouraging appointments on the social front – Marina da Silva as Environment Minister, Cristovam Buarque as Education Minister, and Miguel Rossetto (former vice governor in the PT administration in Rio Grande do Sul and an MST sympathizer) as Minister of Agrarian Reform – it seems unlikely that Lula will be attempting this, at least in the first phase of his government. The new government, it appears, will be settling for the much more modest target of 'humanising' neo-liberalism. This was hinted at in *Fome Zero* where the PT spoke, not of 'growth *through* income redistribution' (that is, making income distribution the engine of growth), but of 'growth *with* income distribution' (that is, economic growth accompanied by measures to redistribute income). This strategy was implicit in Lula's selection of ministers for the powerful economic ministries – Antônio Palocci (a former moderate PT mayor) as Finance Minister, Henrique Meirelles (former head of the global BankBoston) as governor of the Central Bank, Luiz Fernando Furlan (chief executive of Sadia, Brazil's leading chicken exporter and a regular participant in the annual Davos conference) as Minister of Development and Roberto Rodrigues (a leading rural businessman and advocate of GM crops) as Minister of Agriculture. Despite differences between them, all these appointees are orthodox economic thinkers. Lula, it seems, will be attempting to repeat on a national scale the policy adopted by many PT mayors on a local scale – caution and orthodoxy on the economic front, combined with daring and imagination on the social front. It will be a difficult act to pull off.

The new government faces a particularly daunting challenge on the external front, although the problems are more political than strictly economic. Whereas Argentina clung to an overvalued currency until it defaulted on its foreign debt and the whole economy collapsed in December 2001, Brazil devalued in late 1999 while it was still possible to find a less calamitous route out of the crisis. The more competitive *real*, combined with the sluggish economy, which kept imports low, meant that Brazil's trade balance bounced back into the black: in 2001 Brazil had a trade surplus of US$2.6 billion and, in October 2002, the *Economist* Intelligence Unit (EIU) was predicting a trade surplus of US$8.6 billion in 2002, US$13.0 billion in 2003 and, after a modest recovery in imports due to higher growth in the domestic economy, of US$11.5 billion in 2004. This means that in the longer term Brazil may be able to generate enough foreign resources to deal with its foreign commitments and reduce its dependence on foreign finance.

However, it seems almost impossible in the shorter term for the new Brazilian government to regain control over the economy without some kind of confrontation with its foreign creditors. Objectively, Brazil's foreign currency borrowing requirements are not onerous. According to the EIU, Brazil faces medium- and long-term debt repayments of US$23.9 billion in 2003 and US$29.6 billion in 2004. If foreign banks maintain short-term lines at their current level of about US$20 billion, Brazil should, in theory, be able to cover its foreign debt commitments from 2003 from IMF disbursements, scheduled at US$26 billion in 2003. In practice, however, this is unlikely to happen. Foreign banks have long been accustomed to holding Brazil (and other countries) to ransom whenever the government adopts a policy that is not completely to their liking. The mechanism is well known: foreign bankers express 'concern' about economic prospects, investors begin to pull money out of the country, the exchange rate rockets, the country's foreign reserves dwindle, default looms. As the economist Harry Shutt has pointed out, individual countries do not have the foreign resources to stand up to speculators:

> The sheer scale of the funds involved now [on the world's financial market] dwarfs the volumes of reserves at the disposal of governments and central banks seeking to intervene in the market in order to stabilise currency values. This means individual states are increasingly powerless to resist any concerted move by speculators (or even an isolated initiative by one of the larger ones) to push down the value of their currencies.[25]

It is because speculators are so powerful that George Soros made his provocative remark that so annoyed Brazilians about Americans being the people who would really select the next Brazilian president. His comment was widely interpreted in Brazil as being indicative of Soros's overbearing megalomania, but this misses the point; what Soros meant was that Brazil, with its present level of vulnerability, does not have the bargaining power to impose its own economic decisions on a reluctant international financial community. Soros may have been proved technically wrong, in that Brazil elected Lula not Serra, but his point remains apposite: according to his logic, the PT government will only avoid a catastrophic economic crisis, if Lula becomes a Cardoso clone and adopts orthodox economic policies.

There is an alternative, one that Soros does not even consider, but Shutt argues for persuasively:[26] the imposition of capital controls, as both Chile and Malaysia have done success- fully in the past. Such a move would be bitterly opposed by the international financial community, but there are precedents. As the influential left-wing Brazilian economist Luiz Gonzaga Belluzo pointed out in an article in November 2002,[27] the two largest Asian economies – India and China – both have tight capital controls and both economies showed strong per capita annual growth, of 3.7 per cent and 6.4 per cent respectively, throughout the 1990s; during the same period, Brazil and Mexico, the two largest Latin American economies, neither of which had capital controls, grew by 1.0 per cent and 1.2 per cent respectively.

Lula himself is well aware of the need to regain control over the economy. In his first post-victory trip abroad, to Buenos Aires, he commented in a joint press conference with the Argentine president, Eduardo Duhalde:

> Foreign capital is welcome but, in order to overcome economic crises, we have become too dependent on international financial flows and in this way we have lost our capacity to take independent, sovereign decisions. We have been left at the mercy of speculators, who very often don't even know where our countries are situated geographically.

It will be virtually impossible for Brazil to gain prior agreement for such a measures from its foreign creditors, particularly the speculators who currently have such control over financial flows to Brazil. Their attitude can be gauged from the coverage given to Brazil by a leading US market consultant (which charges US$10,000 a year for its reports) during the currency scare in June 2002. After reports that some members of the PT were in favour of a moratorium on the foreign debt, the report cynically (and arrogantly) observed:

> Highly indebted countries do not have the luxury to have a public debate about the desirability of staying current on the debt.... Merely asking the question may make default inevitable.... Brazil's debt profile makes it hard for Brazil to grow and, without growing rapidly, Brazil cannot get out of its debt trap.... Having a former speculator at the helm of the Central Bank [a reference to Armínio

Fraga, president of Brazil's Central Bank during the Cardoso years, who used to work for George Soros] is no guarantee of success, but at least Brazil may be able to avoid some mistakes of the past.

Not surprisingly, the report concluded:

We would not be buying Brazilian debt now, as the higher spreads may provide a bigger cushion against the possibility of default, but they also make default more likely as they increase the pressure on the economy ... the probability of default are [*sic*] high, and if the default doesn't take place now, it will likely happen next time.[28]

The report's advice to its readers was, from its own perspective, quite reasonable, but it highlights starkly the difficulties that the Lula government will face, if it tries to negotiate a way out of the crisis in friendly fashion with foreign creditors.

By the end of the year, the PT's conciliatory rhetoric had changed the foreign image of the new PT government. In October, the *Financial Times* had published a doom-laden editorial in which it stated:

All the hallmarks of an impending defeat are visible: a soaring public service debt burden, high short-term interest rates, low growth, a rapidly depreciating currency, and an international loss of confidence. At current market rates, even an optimist would admit Brazil is insolvent.[29]

By mid-November it was tacitly admitting that its earlier judgement might have been hasty:

There can have been fewer greater surprises this year than the way in which investors have reacted to the presidential election triumph of Luiz Inácio Lula de Silva, the former trades unionist who leads Brazil's left-wing Workers' Party.

Only a few months ago many Wall Street analysts predicted that such an outcome would lead to inevitable default by Brazil on a public debt that in net terms amounted to R$885 billion (US$247 billion) – or 63.9 per cent of gross domestic product – at the end of September.... But in the weeks immediately before and after Mr Lula da Silva's landslide election triumph on October 27, Brazilian asset prices have rallied strongly.

Since the election Brazil's currency has gained 7 per cent and stock prices have risen by 6 per cent in dollar terms. And last month [October] Brazilian bonds generated a total return of about 23 per cent and were the best performing assets as measured by J.P. Morgan's emerging market bond indices.[30]

Foreign bankers are clearly hoping that Lula will be tamed. There is no shortage of Latin American leaders who were elected to power on a fiery, anti-imperialist rhetoric yet changed their tune once in power, dutifully implementing IMF policies: Carlos Andrés Pérez in Venezuela, Alberto Fujimori in Peru, Carlos Menem in Argentina. Maybe Lula will be no different. Perhaps he has already changed for, as was discussed earlier, he campaigned on a sugary, all-inclusive slogan ('Lula, Peace and Love') that is not indicative of steely determination to take on the international financial community. Perhaps the PT will be co-opted by Brazil's wily political elites, which, as Brazilian sociologist José de Souza Martins has long argued, have developed a remarkable skill in taking over social movements:

Since the Second World War all powerful social processes with a real possibility of far-reaching transformation have been changed out of all recognition into projects and solutions which have achieved exactly the opposite of the original objectives of the social struggle. The political system has demonstrated a notable capacity for appropriating pressures and proposals, assimilating and integrating disruptive elements which in other societies have become an essential element in the process leading to profound social and political transformation.[31]

And yet.... There is no doubt that Lula and the PT are different. Lula has always sought negotiation and consensus, even in his early days as a militant labour leader when, to the consternation of his comrades, he invited military representatives to trade union events (see Chapter 2) but, as he also showed at this time, he knows how to fight when negotiations have failed. Moreover, his personal commitment to achieving real social change in Brazil cannot be doubted. And the PT is a strong, organic party, democratic and open, which is committed to radical change and highly resistant to co-option. At the same time, the PT is coming to power at a moment of considerable international uncertainty: while grassroots movements are revolting against neo-liberalism in much of Latin America and the global economy is in turmoil, the United States is aggressively exerting its hegemony as the world's only superpower. In its long history of neo-colonial dependency, Latin America has fared best at moments of continental crisis: Peronism in Argentina and Getulismo in Brazil, both moderately progressive movements in their day, arose in the 1930s when the USA was embroiled in the Great Depression. Never before in its history has Brazil been so deeply enmeshed in the global economic system, yet this too is a double-edged sword for, while foreign capital has much leverage over Brazil, it also has much to lose in a damaging confrontation.

Notes

1 See Fernando Henrique Cardoso, *Mudanças Sociais na América Latina*, Difusão Européia do Livro, São Paulo, 1969; and F. H. Cardoso and Enzo Faletto, *Dependency and Development in Latin America*, Berkeley, 1979.

2 Geisa Maria Rocha, 'Neo-Dependency in Brazil', *New Left Review*, no. 16, July–August 2002, p. 32.

3 Luiz Carlos Bresser-Pereira, 'Financiamento para o Subdesenvolvimento: o Brasil e o Segundo Consenso de Washington', paper presented during the conference commemorating the fiftieth anniversary of the creation of the Banco Nacional de Desenvolvimento Econômico e Social (BNDES), 14 October 2002, p. 15.

4 Rocha, 'Neo-Dependency in Brazil', p. 7.

5   Quoted in ibid., p. 8.

6   Ibid.

7   Harry Shutt, *The Trouble with Capitalism: an Enquiry into the Causes of Global Economic Failure*, Zed Books, London and New York, 1998, p. 82.

8   Rocha, 'Neo-Dependency in Brazil', p. 9.

9   UNCTAD, *World Investment Report 2001*, Country Fact Sheet: Brazil, UNCTAD, Geneva.

10 Bresser-Pereira, 'Financiamento para o Subdesenvolvimento', p. 24.

11 Ibid., p. 19.

12 Rocha, 'Neo-Dependency in Brazil', p. 9.

13 This did not happen when Argentina defaulted in December 2001, as the US government wanted to show it could be tough with 'irresponsible debtors' so did not support a further bail-out; but even then the foreign banks did not bear heavy losses, as the Argentine collapse was so widely predicted that foreign banks had already taken out most of their money by the time it actually happened.

14 Figures from IPEA (Instituto de Pesquisa Econômica Aplicada).

15 This programme was implemented by the then Health Minister, José Serra, later to run as the ruling party's presidential candidate in the 2002 election. Serra's tough stance on Brazil's right to produce its own generic drugs greatly angered the powerful US pharmaceutical multinationals. In 2002 several US newspapers reported that the US administration was more hostile to Serra than to Lula, who had earned grudging respect within the US tradition of self-made men.

16 See chapter 9 in Sue Branford and Jan Rocha, *Cutting the Wire: the Story of the Landless Movement in Brazil*, Latin America Bureau, London, 2002.

17 Figures from Instituto Brasileiro de Geografia e Estadística (IBGE).

18 Quoted in Altamiro Borges, 'A Regressão do Trabalho na "Era FHC",' *Revista Mensal*, year 2, no. 16, September 2002.

19 Ibid.

20 Ibid.

21 Ibid.

22 *Folha de S. Paulo*, 13 May 2001.

23 ECLAC, *Social Panorama*, Table 11.2, pp. 70–1.

24 Instituto Cidadania, *Projeto Fome Zero – Uma Proposta de Politica de Segurança Alimentar para o Brasil*, São Paulo, October 2001, p. 10.

25 Harry Shutt, *The Trouble with Capitalism*, p. 82.

26 Harry Shutt, *A New Democracy: Alternatives to a Bankrupt World Order*, Global Issues Series, Zed Books, London and New York, 2001.

27 *Folha de S. Paulo*, 1 November 2002.

28 *Bridgewater Daily Observations*, 17 June 2002.

29   *Financial Times*, 15 October 2002.
30   *Financial Times*, 10 November 2002.
31   José de Souza Martins, *O Poder do Atraso – Ensaios de Sociologia da História Lenta*, Editora Hucitec, São Paulo, 1999, p. 13.

4

Porto Alegre: Public Power beyond the State*

HILARY WAINWRIGHT

Right from the time it was founded in the early 1980s, the PT has maintained that electoral success is not an end in itself but a springboard for developing radical, participatory forms of democracy that will enable the country to start redressing the enormous inequalities in Brazilian society. The city where the PT has made most advances in this sense is the city of Porto Alegre, the capital of the southern state of Rio Grande do Sul, which has been continuously governed by the PT ever since the charismatic *gaúcho* bank clerk, Olívio Dutra, was first elected mayor in 1989.

Throughout the 21 years of military rule (1964–85) Porto Alegre was a centre of resistance. The city's neighbourhood associations, which now are at the root of the administration's main innovation, the so-called *orçamento participativo* (participatory budget), provided refuge for persecuted dissidents, and later became an important source of support for the PT. Even before the 1989 election of Dutra, these neighbourhood associations (*associações de bairro*) and other urban movements in the city were demanding the democratisation of local government, the ending of corruption and the opening up of budget decision making. In some ways, Porto Alegre is not a typical Brazilian city, for it has always had an unusually high literacy rate, even before the reforms of the 1990s (in 1991 it was 96 per cent, well above the Brazilian average of 81 per cent). But it has not bucked the Brazilian trend of extreme social inequality: in 1981 one third of the city's people lived in slum areas. At the same time, 15 families own almost all the urban land available for development.

In Porto Alegre, as throughout Brazil, municipal state departments and their leading officials had vested interests in this inequality. Corruption was endemic. The local PT believed that the only chance of achieving change was to open up these secretive municipal institutions, particularly their finances, to a process of popular participation. So when the PT gained control of the municipal government, it invited citizens to participate in the decisions about the city's new investments. It calls this the *orçamento participativo*, or 'participatory budget' (PB). PB is a form of co-decision making or shared power. Through a process of meetings in which they elect delegates, citizens decide on the priorities for the municipal investment budget. They argue for the relative importance of investment in projects of public works, services and the social economy. But the principle of popular participation has spread more widely through the city's administration. 'Participation is addictive', says Betânia Alfonsin, a young urban planner who used to be in the local leadership of the PT and now works with movements in the *favelas* (shanty-towns).

The particular combination in Porto Alegre of well-organised urban movements, strong democratic traditions and a history of left-of-centre governments provided good conditions in which to test out the PT's new, still undefined ideas of participation. Even before 1989, there was pressure from neighbourhood movements in the city for greater democracy in finances. In 1985, 300 delegates attended the founding congress of the city-wide UAMPA (Union of Residents' Associations) where they drew up a draft proposal for opening up the budgetary process. The drawing up and submission of this proposal flexed a new kind of muscle which took urban grassroots organisation beyond purely parochial concerns and laid the basis for city-wide popular participation. The proposal to open up the city's budget in this way played a large part in creating the atmosphere in which, when Dutra won office, it made sense for him to discuss with the popular movements of the city themselves how his government should cope with the municipality's financial difficulties. In this way, his administration broke with the previous tradition by which the elected government tied up deals among the political elite. From the start, the PT allowed the ordinary people of Porto Alegre, especially the poorer people, to become a source of power in the government of the city. They became the central dynamic force influencing the decisions of the municipal legislature, in which no one party had a majority.

At a first glance, it would seem that conditions in Porto Alegre were uniquely favourable to the emergence of PB, but similar ideas had also taken root in the completely different conditions of Santo André, part of the industrial belt around the city of São Paulo that had been the birthplace of the PT and was, until the 1990s, one the largest car manufacturing centres in the world. There the grassroots democracy of CUT, the leading left-wing trade union confederation, was fertile ground for ideas of popular participation in financial decision making. CUT was created by industrial workers in the early 1980s to give them independent bargaining strength at a time when the official unions, from the moment of the 1964 military coup onwards, 'just said yes', in the words of João Avamileno, the city's vice-mayor, a founder member of CUT. For him the idea of basing the municipal budget on popular participation followed logically from the way decisions were taken over CUT's budget: 'The workers in each union, through their local and regional assemblies, would discuss and decide their priorities for the whole organisation. These participatory methods are essential.'

The replication of apparently specific conditions is perhaps a sign that sharing decision making over municipal money taps into a collective democratic inventiveness – potentially a universal phenomenon. The connection between opening up the black hole of state finance and stimulating the growth of a popular democratic power was partially anticipated in new thinking in the Workers' Party, but it was not a fully developed part of its programme. From the mid-1980s, as the PT started standing in elections, the party began to debate how to use office to achieve the radical transformation for which it was working through social movements. Celso Daniel, an intellectual and activist with a profound commitment to deepening democracy, who became mayor of Santo André, was part of those debates. He explained to me the thinking that led to PB: 'We believed in taking the principles of democracy from social movements, including the trade union movement, with us when we gained office. That meant we had to share political power, the management of the city, with the community.' Finance is power, Daniel believed, so opening the budget was the best test of the sharing of power.

Daniel believed that these principles, so far applied only at municipal and state government level, have implications for the federal government, something that has gained a new relevance with Lula's victory:

> It's very important to try to build a regionalised central budget, because the differences between regions are huge, so if the President of Brazil becomes committed to the participatory budget process at the central level, this could be very important for the construction of a new kind of federalism in Brazil.

He explained how the present federal system in Brazil is 'very tied to the old oligarchies, the old elites in Brazil'. Daniel, who was a close Lula adviser, would undoubtedly have held a key position in the PT government had he not been murdered in January 2002; he is one of several PT mayors killed, probably by members of a drugs mafia threatened by the new open method of government. He was a prophetic thinker as well as a brave leader.

I myself was curious to explore whether the PB has an even

wider international relevance. This is how I found myself aboard a flight from Rio's Santos Dumont airport, clutching the Rough Guide to Brazil in one hand and the rather more glossy Prefeitura guide to PB in Porto Alegre in the other, my hand luggage stuffed to over-spilling with selections from the growing literature on the PT and the PB, including Canadian political historian Margaret Keck's classic book on the PT,[1] articles by Portuguese sociologist Boaventura de Souza Santos and texts by the prolific philosopher, lawyer and twice-elected mayor of Porto Alegre, Tarso Genro.

The participatory tourist

Porto Alegre, capital city of the relatively wealthy state of Rio Grande do Sul, is a busy industrial, financial and service centre with a population of 1.2 million people and, judging by the crowded bus station, many more who commute into the city from the countryside. It has become an international city not by prostrating itself at the feet of predatory corporations in the hope of inward investment, but, ironically, because it has become internationally renowned for 'good government'. For political, cultural and economic reasons, it nurtures this reputation. There are cheap flats especially available for the steady stream of curious visitors.

It was not long since Peter Mandelson, a former minister close to the UK's Tony Blair, had been touring Brazil, showering some of New Labour's electoral glory on to President Cardoso and castigating the PT as 'old-fashioned', but no one held the behaviour of this dubious fellow-countryman against me. To my surprise, a polite young man met me at the airport and took me to a municipal car emblazoned with the logo in Portuguese – 'Porto Alegre, the city where participation makes democracy'. I had expected to have to hunt down the participatory budget: in fact it had come to greet me. My guide introduced himself as Vinicius. In previous weeks, he had been assisting representatives from the Inter-American Development Bank and the UN, and delegations from other Brazilian and international municipalities keen to learn and exchange.

On the way to my first interview the participatory car paused to pick up Isabella, who was to translate for me. Her father had been a brave senior pilot who opposed the military coup. After refusing to carry out a mission, he was murdered in circumstances that remain mysterious. The memory of the dictatorship and the fight for democracy are still potent. It was formative in the political outlook of many of the activists I met on my tour of the participatory process. Isabella was one of them.

The Budget Planning Office, GAPLAN

We drove first to meet the man at the head of the government's side of the participatory process, the Gabinete de Planejamento – the budget planning committee or GAPLAN, as it is known in the acronym alphabet of PB. I must have imagined a grey-suited, probably grey-haired mandarin, because I was surprised by the friendly, tanned young man, suit-less and tie-less, who greeted me. This was André Passos, a 30-year-old economist and a PT member since the age of 15, now chief of the Budget Planning Department in GAPLAN. His office was full of posters announcing political meetings and seminars. Part of his job is to explain the conclusions of his technical work to the citizen participants, so his political commitment to the process is important. Later in the week I was to observe him reporting back to a 600-strong plenary, answering tough questions and fielding persistent criticisms at a typically argumentative meeting of the COP (Conselho do Orçamento Participativo), the elected council for the participatory budget.

Legally, André Passos is employed by the mayor, but his job faces both ways. At certain points in the budgetary cycle he explains and persuades on behalf of the government, to the people. At other moments in the cycle he scrutinises, on behalf of the people, the activities of the government. He co-ordinates the 'technical criteria' for the budget, that is the legal, physical and financial constraints that it must work within. His technical word is not taken as gospel, however. For example, three years into the process, movements in the *favelas* challenged the government's claim that it had no power to legalise or 'regularise' their rights over the land they had squatted. The government had been doing its best to provide sewerage, electricity and water to the squatted residences but this was not enough for the tenants who, with the advice of radical NGOs and law students, successfully insisted that the municipality regularise their living conditions, using up-to-then unused provisions in the progressive, post-military 1988 constitution. Ten years later, the regularisation is complete, carried out under new local legislation, approved to enact the constitutional measure and considered one of the most progressive laws in Brazil.

André works as a servant of the public. He is powerful but not personally so; his power derives from both the mandate of the mayor and the authority of the participatory process. His work reveals how PB influences the day-to-day operations of what in Britain would be the department of the city council's chief executive – though because of Brazil's mayoral system the comparison is not straightforward. Over its 15 years, the PB has opened up a state bureaucracy that is normally hidden. Such openness repels what are often corrupt pressures on council departments from private interests. Before PB, such interests regularly short-circuited the democratic process.

There are serious constraints on the scope of the PB. If you consider general, country-wide taxation, 57–59 per cent goes to the federal government, 27–28 per cent to the state level and 14 per cent remains at the municipal level. There are some additional taxes collected by the municipality and they can be changed by municipal laws. At present, or at least up to the new presidency, the trend is towards the municipality increasing its responsibilities (especially concerning new social services) but concentrating revenue from taxation with the federal government – a nifty device which helps central government pay the external and internal debt and leaves social problems in the hands of increasingly constrained municipalities.

Porto Alegre council collects 10–20 per cent of its total revenue through local taxes; the rest comes from federal and state grants. As federal law stipulates that 57 per cent of the city's local tax revenue must go back to the federal government, and another 27 per cent be spent on health and on education, Porto Alegre is left with 16 per cent of local tax revenue, as well as grants from the federal and state governments. In 1989, nearly 90 per cent of the budget went on salaries, with few funds – less than 10 per cent – left for new investments, even in basics like sewerage, pavements, new schools or health centres. Now 15 per cent of the budget each year is spent on new investments.

Porto Alegre City Council is permitted to increase its revenue through municipal enterprises. André stresses the future importance of this, pointing to an information technology company that was originally created to serve public departments and now offers its services more widely. The increased revenue goes back into the company and will enable it to invest in optical fibre technology, which will be a future source of revenue. The city's water company is also municipally owned, and most of Porto Alegre's buses are built by a highly successful company owned by the city council. There is also a growing network of municipally owned but cooperatively run recycling projects – all this at a time when elsewhere in the world governments and corporations try to persuade us that 'modernisation' means privatisation.

Here then in André Passos' offices, more like a students union than a British-style town hall, is a new local government institution. It has centralised power over all municipal government departments but its job is to ensure that these departments respond to the priorities set 'from below'. It was reminiscent, to me, of the 'programme office' at the Greater London Council under Ken Livingstone. This also was an innovation: its job was to monitor and ensure that all GLC departments carried out the manifesto on which the leadership of the GLC was elected. But GAPLAN's role was far more active than this: it was not simply following up the electoral mandate of one day's voting but servicing a year-long process of democratic participation.

Civil power and the transformative vision of Paulo Freire

Many of those who theorise about the participative process, most notably Tarso Genro, the lawyer-philosopher who became mayor after Olívio Dutra, refer to the emergence of a new source of democratic civil power independent of the state. Genro says that there are now two focal points of democratic power: one originating from the vote; and the other from institutions of direct democracy. How does this new form of power actually work on the ground? How far does the participatory process have an independence that enables it genuinely to be a source of power over the state? What difference does it make to the state's responsiveness to the needs of the people? And how does it avoid privileging just the needs of the most articulate and well-organised – becoming just a new, more public form of corruption?

It is impossible to understand the participatory methods of the PT without recognising the important contribution made by Paulo Freire's ideas on education. A supporter of the PT until he died in 1997, Freire saw education as a transformative tool that could create experiences of a truly equal and democratic nature, which people would then be inspired to reproduce. He had observed the way we ape and imitate traditional relation-ships of power and then reproduce them when we ourselves gain any kind of power. The goal of his education was to break this pattern and thus obstruct the reproduction of established power. His emphasis on cultural, as well as political and economic, transformation is echoed in the PT's participative methods of government. The PT does not simply seek to get into office, occupy the driving seat and drive the machinery of state towards the poor. Rather, it aims, in municipalities like Porto Alegre, to open up the state machinery and involve all citizens – the poor especially – in deciding how it should work, a collaborative process that is both personally and socially transformative. Such transformations need constant cultural nourishment too.

The Freire model of education as transformation provides an insight into the paradox of a process, facilitated by the government, which produces a form of citizens' power that is a democratic check on the apparatus of the state. PB is coordinated by the local government, just as a Freirian teacher coordinates the education process – in both cases frameworks are open to change and in both cases it is assumed that citizens have their own demands, organisation and knowledge. Thus, just as the teacher assumes that 'students' already have knowledge, and treats education as a collaboration, so it was always part of the PT's political understanding that it would share with the community whatever power it gained through electoral success, and be open to their knowledge too.

The office for coordinating relations with the community

We drove next through the port area of the city to a converted bus depot, where the offices of the Coordenação de Relações com as Comunidades (the Coordination Committee for Relations with the Community, CRC) are located. This is where the influence of Freire's fusion of education and political transformation was most evident. After walking through a series of somewhat chaotic offices, reminiscent of a leaflet warehouse, we reached Assis Brasil, the jovial and universally flirtatious head of CRC, who invited us to sit down and talk with him and some of the regional PB coordinators.

There are 20 coordinators, one for each region of the city and four working on particular themes: women, youth, black people and older people. Assis introduced me to those who were hanging round the office, picking up leaflets. Some of the people we met had been priests – the influence of radical Catholicism is pervasive amongst the PT and its supporters; some, amongst the women especially, had trained to join a religious order as a way of gaining education and getting out of the *favelas*, but left before taking their final vows; others had been active in the neighbourhood movements, fighting for the legislation of squatted land or for sewerage or rubbish collection; several had been active in the landless movement before coming to the city; and a few were committed intellectuals, teachers and academics.

In the first 15 years of the PT's administration, the CRC has played a crucial role in organising PB. The CRC coordinators' most important role is working with the PB delegates elected by the first regional PB plenaries. In practice, the PB coordinators help the PB delegates through three tasks. First, there are the discussions with technical people from the town hall about the practicalities of different improvements; second, there are neighbourhood meetings to develop proposals and hear people's views on them; and third, there is the drawing up of a hierarchy of priorities to put to their region's second plenary and from there to the budgetary council. These three tasks are the responsibility of the delegates and the community. Even though local government does not co-manage this part of the process, the coordinators have the responsibility of making sure that people have access to technical information and of helping groups to communicate with each other, so that delegates, having to choose between competing priorities, can understand the needs of the region as a whole. In one region, Restinga, they had nearly 50 community meetings during this vital intermediary period, before arriving at their priorities. 'Coordinators vary', said Luciano Brunet. In the 1970s he was part of the student movement resisting the dictatorship before he and his strong feminist partner, Helene, became founding members of the PT; today he works closely with Assis. 'Their role depends a lot on how strong and confident the local organisations are. Some coordinators encourage the community to be really innovative.' At one stage, there were complaints of coordinators becoming too involved and undermining the independence of the local organisations. 'Because of this', explains Luciano, 'there's an unwritten rule that regional coordinators do not live in the region where they work or, if they do, they are not personally involved in the local organisations.'

The more Luciano explained the inner realities of the CRC and the work of the coordinators, the more it seemed that, while André's department was the technical engine-room of PB, the CRC was its social and political fuel injection system. The vital role of the PB coordinators in Porto Alegre contrasts starkly with recent British experience, where local authorities, under national pressure, have cut to the point of elimination their community development and adult education teams. The Brazilian example contains salutary lessons for any strategy of genuine community involvement. In Porto Alegre, genuine citizen participation in decision making is taken seriously. The work of PB coordinators is crucial to the development of people's power to control the local state. They have to be extremely skilled, exerting authority with government departments, and at the same time teaching ordinary people to develop their own power and capacity to organise.

Mapping the whole process

After an afternoon with the government's budget committee

and the following morning with community coordinators, I began to get a clearer grasp of the whole process. The mechanisms of the PB are clear, though complex and original. There is a cycle of three types of PB meetings annually – regional and thematic plenaries, forums of regional delegates, and the budget council (the COP). The first round of plenary meetings, held in each of the 16 regions of the city, takes place in March. These plenaries focus on the previous year's spending. Government officials, flanked by citizens' delegates, explain the timing and quality of the delivery of the actions agreed by the neighbourhood the year before. Has it gone according to plan? This first plenary in the year also elects regional delegates for the next stage in the process: the delegates' forums, at which each region will establish its priorities.[2] This is where the CRC's PB coordinators' work can be vital. In addition, this first plenary elects two city delegates to be members of the COP.

Before the regional delegates take decisions about regional priorities, they meet with their groups to seek out their views on areas, such as road building, schools, health provision, sewerage, economic development including cooperatives, and leisure and sports facilities. The regional delegates meet together monthly, or more often, to work out the proposed priorities for the region. The delegates then gather together at the delegates' forum, where they work out budget priorities for their region by combining two objective criteria (population size and statistically measured need) with one subjective criterion (the priority given to different issues by the community). They apply a weighting system so that quantitative weights can be given to different areas of investment. The same criteria are applied across the city. This weighting system, sometimes known as the 'budget matrix', plays a crucial role in creating awareness of the needs of both the different regions and of the city as a whole.

The municipal government also holds plenaries around themes, bringing together people from across the city with a common interest: for example, education, health, culture, economics. These important thematic plenaries also elect delegates to the COP, which starts meeting in July or August. The COP is a powerful body that negotiates the final investment priorities for the city, on the basis of input from the regions and the thematic groups. In addition, it considers some projects proposed by the government itself. Through an open process of negotiation and reporting back, the COP draws up the overall budget and puts it to the mayor and municipal council for final agreement.

People's plenaries: accountability and vision

I was able to see this co-management in action myself at a plenary on my second evening in Porto Alegre. It was the opening meeting of the 2001 budgetary process in the Northern zone. Our taxi sped northwards, over smooth roads, past numerous construction projects. Isabella and I were dropped off behind a fleet of minibuses in sight of a long queue to the entrance of the building where the meeting was to be held. The CRC's budget coordinators put on the minibuses for people with no transport. As people entered the meeting, they registered: name, address, the name of their association, even it was only an informal street organisation they were part of. Registration is important for several reasons. One is that it counts the number of people at the meeting, which today is the basis on which participants elect their delegates. At first, a very simple method was used: one delegate per 5 people at the meeting, then one per 10, then one per 20, as involvement in PB meetings grew (from 1,000 in 1990, to 3,700 in 1991, to 10,000 in 1993, to 20,000 in 1997 and now to around 40,000). But finally, in 1997, the COP had to change the rules to make sure that all areas of the city are represented, even those where people are not very active. Now meetings with an attendance of up to 100 choose one delegate for every 10 people; meetings with an attendance of 101–1,000 choose one for every 70; and meetings of more than 1,000 choose one for every 80.

The school that hosted the assembly provided the whole ground floor for registration but it still took time. While people waited, a troupe of actors put on a kind of street theatre, focusing on local problems. To an outsider, the people streaming in seemed to be a cross-section of the whole of the community: white-haired matrons; eager schoolgirls; young rasta men; the anxious poor, often black; glamorous young student types with a tan; confident-looking middle aged men of various shades of brown. But the coordinators said that some neighbourhoods were much better represented than others and this was another reason for the registration, for it enabled them to identify areas, or groups of people, that were not well represented and find out why. Around 600 people had come, out of a community of 3,000. The majority attending that night were women.

If the structure of the cycle of meetings is PB's blueprint, it is the participants themselves who give it life. During meetings there is an opportunity not only to protest and let off steam, but also to explore needs and propose solutions. A statistical survey of the participation of different social groups by CIDADE, an independent research organisation, shows that a large majority of the participants are unskilled workers with only a primary level of education. Women, too, are very well represented: over the last four years there have been more women than men at the plenaries, and more women than men have been elected delegates. This is impressive for a region that is renowned throughout Brazil for its *machismo*. And, in a city that until recently excluded black people from the main supermarkets and from factory jobs, it is particularly noteworthy that at least a quarter of the delegates to the COP are black or indigenous people. PB meetings have become a focal point for people previously excluded from the political process.

The people crowding into the vast school hall saw the meeting as an opportunity to vent their feelings to government representatives, as well as to win over their neighbours in support of their chosen causes. A local tradition of public story-telling makes for a hall full of vivid narrators of tales of municipal failings, and two groups were particularly vociferous. In the previous year's budget, sanitation had been a high priority but, complained speaker after speaker, the problems of dirty water and open sewers remained, even though a lot of money had been spent on the area. People from one neighbourhood complained about a stream that had become the local sewer, saying that they wanted it closed over so it could not be used in this way. Government officials at the meeting said that, for environmental reasons, the stream should remain a stream but they promised to clean it. Another vocal group were from a local school. They had come to a budget plenary for the first time and used it simply to shout out their complaints. The Mayor, Raoul Pont, responded, urging them to elect a delegate, turn their complaints into proposals and negotiate for funds through PB.

On the platform at the front of the hall sat a mixture of people, some from the municipality's executive departments, some from the community. Alongside the mayor was André Passos, next to him Luciano from the CRC; from the community there were the current delegates to the COP from this region, as well as two *vereadores* – that is, the elected members of the municipal legislative assembly for the area. Once the long queue of people registering had snaked its way into the hall and we were settling down in our seats, the chair asked for an indication of how many were attending their first PB meeting. Over 300 hands went up. This is quite common; new people are constantly engaging with the process. Despite hostile local media, recent surveys show that over 85 per cent of Porto Alegrans know about and support PB. They find out about it through their neighbours and friends, through leaflets and through delegates, like the ones they were about to elect at this meeting. PB itself has become a form of media.

Later in my visit I discussed these plenaries with Eduardo

Utzig, who, as a social researcher and a former senior government official (when Tarso Genro was mayor), has a comprehensive and reflective understanding of the process. He said that the PB's influence has grown. 'The people notice if works are late and the delegates put pressure on the government, "Why is there a delay?" they ask. And, if the problem isn't solved, they mobilise the community and bring them into the city hall.' Utzig certainly felt he had been under constant direct popular pressure when he was in government, and he thought this made him more efficient. He said that the pressure does not come in a form that officials can easily control, for there is no single formal procedure. It can be direct to government departments, to the mayor, through the budget council or through the regional PB coordinators.

The rules and criteria for PB are mathematically precise and treated with great seriousness by government and community alike. Rules for the participatory budgeting process are written up as a handbook, 'Procedures of the Participatory Budget', which is annually revised, reflecting the continuing process of refinement and adaptation. All 600 or so people attending a plenary meeting have a copy. Thus PB is a self-reproducing and self-regulating process, with formalised mechanisms for learning, monitoring and adapting.

The people's delegates

The main role of the delegates elected at the first plenaries is to sound people out and to listen. Delegates bring the result of these visits to regular meetings for preparing the region's priorities. They also meet together throughout the year to iron out problems, monitor progress, and encourage ideas for next year's budget. And they keep in regular touch with the region's two representatives on the COP. These COP representatives are accountable to the regional delegates and could in theory be recalled by a specially convened plenary, though this has yet to happen. This notion of recall, or 'retorno', is an important one in the participatory process, demonstrating the accountability of representatives on the powerful budget council, the apex of the whole process.

Delegates at both the regional and the city level are regularly under pressure from their electors. Listen to Jussara Bechstein-Silva (hybrid German–Brazilian names are common in a city which was host to large migrations from Europe in the late nineteenth century, especially from Germany and Italy), who represents the central region on the COP. She is a forceful charismatic leader in Vila Planetário, fighting for the land to be regularised and its present residents to remain in the centre of the city. She found it hard being a COP representative. 'You have to answer to the local inhabitants who are asking: "Why is it so delayed? Why is it failing?" And you have to answer to the council too. You are pressured on both sides.' But she felt supported: 'The mayor, Olívio Dutra, came one night in the pouring rain and told us to be hopeful because the construction would be completed. And we had a lot of support from our lawyer' – a woman who worked in the planning department, part of whose job was to provide technical support for the community.

The openness of the election of delegates can be hijacked. In one region, the system was manipulated by a private company, who paid people to attend the plenary and to elect delegates supportive of their business interests. The other delegates realised what was going on and the ensuing conflicts ended in the police station. The longer-term result was a system of very tough rules to guard against such abuse: for example, any delegate who misses more than three meetings has to be replaced, which minimises the extent to which people get elected simply to lobby for a single project.

The Budget Council, COP

Finally, all that remained to be visited was the COP itself. In most modern societies important meetings are closed or, if they are formally open, they are in practice surrounded by so much red tape that they might as well be closed. But in the *petista* version of Brazilian culture, it seems everything is open (just about: there must be some closed doors somewhere). So, along with at least two other international visitors, I and Isabella sat in on a COP meeting. It was held in the same rather non-descript municipal building where André Passos had his office. There were about 20 city delegates there – a full attendance would be over 40 delegates – with only two members of the government. It is revealing that, though the majority of people who attend the open plenaries are women, the majority of the 20 or so COP delegates attending this meeting were men. Two were black, most were mixed-race, and there was one deaf man and his signer. At the desk in front sat André, Assis and two community representatives, one of whom took the chair.

By April, preparation of the budget proposal and the Investment Plan is complete. Proposals are submitted to the municipal assembly in December and agreed by the mayor the next February. So the meeting we attended in June dealt with concerns outside the main priorities. Discussion focused on a sports hall here, some cultural activity there. There were some complaints and some questions. Even though the agenda was not as important as at some meetings, it was a rumbustious affair. André and Assis, as government representatives, were put on the spot mercilessly. At one point, halfway through a hot and gruelling meeting, they were both out of the room. Delegates smelt a caucus of the two officials and, to retrieve their position, Assis bounced back. 'Can't a man have a piss?' he joked.

Betânia Alfonsin, the urban planner who works closely with neighbourhood groups in areas like Vila Planetário and has a long experience of the PB, said she had been impressed by the COP meetings. 'I was surprised. I felt these people are doing far more for the city than we do in our departments.' And they are doing it unpaid. Even though COP meetings take place for two hours every week, all year round (except February), and twice a week in the period from September until November (when the investment plan is decided), delegates receive no payment whatsoever. 'The whole system of the participatory budget runs off militancy', explains Valério Lopes, the president of the financial committee of UAMPA, the city's network of neighbourhood associations. 'The only people who receive payment are the municipal workers related to the process. The delegates have to take care of all their expenses, including bus tickets or petrol.'

The overall budget for 2001 was R$600 million (about US$230 million), of which R$90 million was available for new investments, to be decided through PB, then ratified by the mayor and finally proposed to the municipal legislature (*Câmara de Vereadores*). At this point André Passos and his colleagues can introduce into the discussion government proposals that target the whole city, proposals that have not been through the PB system. One popular City Congress proposal was the redevelopment of the closed market into an attractive multi-use public centre. Such proposals do not automatically get accepted now, although they used to in the early days. 'People didn't have the information the government had and they weren't able to discuss on equal terms', commented Sérgio Baerlie, a long-time observer of the process. He drew an important conclusion: 'Sometimes it's not enough to have the opportunity to decide, if you don't have the instruments – such as the information and consciousness – to debate on equal terms.' Delegates debate on more equal terms now than they did at first: 'People don't simply accept the budget proposals brought by the government', says Sérgio. 'They start comparing with previous years. They have the documents to do so. They have learnt. They start questioning why something else got more money than the top priority of the participatory process. Increasingly, the government has to justify itself.' Being on the COP is a steep learning curve and, in order for the expertise and confidence accruing from the experience to be shared as widely as possible, seats on the COP are rotated. No one can be a COP member, or a substitute, for more that two consecutive years; though someone can stand again after two years off.

Between September and December comes a particularly intensive period in the life of a COP delegate. This is when the detailed Investment Plan is drawn up, listing the works and activities chosen for that year. The municipal chamber has never rejected the COP's budget or made any damaging amendments. The Investment Plan is published annually as a vital reference document, which all regional and thematic delegates refer to as they supervise the departments carrying out the work. The government uses the Plan when it is called to account by any organ of the participatory budget.

Something missing

There are problems, however. Betânia Alfonsin:

> The budgetary process is not enough. The COP is very powerful but it only deals with investments. You cannot plan a city just on the basis of individual investments. We have to complement it by democratising and strengthening urban planning. If not, you can get a gulf between city planning and specific investments. An example of this lack of coordination was the expansion of the sewerage network, which now covers more than 80 per cent of the city. This work was not accompanied by an investment in water treatment, which has resulted in a considerable increase of untreated sewerage flowing into the city's main water source, Lake Guaíba.

There are two related issues here. One is that planning and policy have not caught up with the dynamic reality of the participatory budget. The planning department used to be the centre of power in the old administration. It was centralised finance, the city's 'works department', one super department responsible for infrastructure and planning. The PT administration broke this up in order to carry out their democratic reforms, and resentment has lingered on. Key professional staff in the depleted planning department have been on what is essentially a long-term 'go slow'. The other is that government departments are fragmented and uncoordinated. There is pressure from PB plenaries in some regions for the government to set up regular dialogue between departments.

In Porto Alegre, improving the efficiency of government is not the process familiar to anyone working today in local government in the UK – the setting of tougher targets at the top and the tightening of the control structure in the hope that those below deliver. In the city of participatory democracy, this is turned on its head, for it has become almost axiomatic to connect efficiency with democracy. 'We have to democratise urban planning, and we have to do so in a comprehensive way', says Betânia. Government leaders are aware of this problem and have encouraged the urban planning department to embark on a major new initiative in participation. How will the new participatory structure for urban planning link to the PB? 'I'm not sure. I don't think the government know either.' There are signs in some areas, however, that this participatory planning is already feeding directly into the budget process, even becoming the basis on which delegates choose priorities.

Under siege

The integration of urban planning and other policy areas with the PB, and the development of a stronger, participatory approach to policy issues other than new investments have become urgent priorities. As was discussed earlier in this book, the federal government has opened the national economy to the full, unrestrained impact of global deregulation, with the concomitant pressures to privatise and run down the state's social capacities. As a result, the federal government has strengthened central control over public spending and has cut the funds going back to the cities whose citizens pay the taxes.

Funds going to local authorities were reduced from 17 per cent of the revenue received in 1990 to 14 per cent in 1999. Further cuts have happened since then.

Porto Alegre cannot put up a Chinese wall, however good its policies on job creation, health, education, infrastructure and social security. It is under siege, part of the front line of a global economic and political war. Almost every reflex in the city's strengthened body politic has moved in the opposite direction to that of the federal state and indeed of most governments across the world. On the whole, governments have willingly reduced their capacity to meet the needs of their poor by, for example, cutting public spending and lowering taxes on the rich. The Popular Administration of Porto Alegre has moved against this stream, expanding its ability to fulfil its citizens' social rights by increasing its revenue through redistributive taxation, and setting up a decision-making process deliberately responsive to the needs of the poor. The power of PB has inverted the priorities of the federal government, and in the area of new investments, where the municipality has control, it has redistributed in favour of the poor. But the PB alone cannot adequately protect against federal policies that destroy the economic ground on which its commitment to social justice stands. All it can do is engage in the wider political struggle for federal and global change – something it does with great verve and considerable human and political resources. In the meantime, there has been not only the misery of livelihoods destroyed by political decisions taken by Fernando Henrique Cardoso in the comfort of the presidential palace in Brasília, but also the danger that the Popular Administration itself could become unintentionally complicit in imposing on local communities the burden of clearing up the unregulated market's social mess.

Not by investment decisions alone

Essentially, the logic goes like this. Against the background just described, poor communities face greater and greater social problems. Their needs intensify. In the meantime, the municipal council's budget to help meet these needs is cut. Its capacity for providing high-quality free services, such as childcare, health, education and housing, is reduced. Local communities put forward projects for solving these problems themselves. The participatory budget agrees with these grassroots solutions, for they fit the basic budget criteria. But what is not discussed is the quality of the service, the level of pay, how the project connects with services provided directly by the municipality, whether the need could be met in better ways, how it will be supervised to ensure that it is providing high-quality services. Sérgio Baerlie illustrates this problem with the example of community day-care centres.

> The money that the municipal government needs to run by itself just one day-care centre is enough to fund several, perhaps more than ten, day-care centres run by community associations, where labour costs are much lower. The result is that today Porto Alegre has 118 day-care centres run by community associations with funds from city hall.

Baerlie suggests there is a danger here of unintentionally accepting a neo-liberal transfer of social policy from the state to the community and in the process undermining the principle of the provision of free public services as a universal social right.

Sérgio Baerlie has other concerns too:

> While agreements between city hall and community organisations are public and are processed on the basis of suggestions from the people, a significant number of management issues tend to be left out of public discussion. For example: how can it be guaranteed that the professionals who are hired are not relatives of the leader of the community organisation? How do we approach the fact that parents often still have to pay for the service? In that case, what is a fair price? Why must some parents pay and others not, since in the few municipal day-care centres no monthly fee is charged? In other words, how can it be ensured that public money is managed in a

transparent fashion and with the agreement of parents and the community.

He is stressing that it is not enough to seek to democratise the state but that social institutions outside the state must also democratise themselves, and this applies to the kinds of independent projects that are funded through the PB. 'No one would suggest ending agreements such as the community day-cares initiative, yet without a democratic transformation of their management, there is no challenge to the neo-liberal "common sense".' The other danger is that, as private corporations increasingly involve themselves, not without self-interest, in the funding of different aspects of the 'social economy' from childcare to recycling, community organisations will lose autonomy, becoming less able to stand up for the rights and needs of their communities. They will become in effect minnows keeping the water clean for the big fish.

There is a growing feeling amongst politically minded government officials, NGO researchers and PB delegates that policy and strategy, as distinct from simply the priorities for the investment budget, need to be both deepened and integrated. There is active support for popular processes of urban planning and economic development, as well as pressure on city hall departments to integrate their policy. Part of the answer seems to be to extend the participatory process of decision making – beyond the bi-annual City Congresses, which are more consultative than decision-making – into policy development. Debates and changes are under way. Aspects of the popular administration are unusually self-reflexive for a public body, but then they are unusual public bodies. The COP, most notably, is able to learn from its failings and change. There is also an openness to criticism at the heart of the government, which is always a good sign and a contrast to the defensiveness so often to be found in many political authorities. For example, the mayor's office organised a seminar so that international researchers could share their criticisms.

All dressed up and nowhere to go: the party seeks a new direction

Traditionally the party, in this case the PT, would play the leadership role in the formation of policy and strategy for the city. It would be the party that would choose a direction, stay a step or two ahead, collectively develop a clear vision, and be, in effect, the brains behind the process. But PB has a problem, born of success: the process of participatory budgeting has proved unpredictable. In contrast to the conventional model of a party controlling, or perceiving itself to control, a state apparatus, PB has unleashed a more potent, more broadly based, means of controlling at least a central part of the state. Instead of monopolising the role of conscious political brain, it has encouraged many political 'brains', many self-conscious agents of social change. This implicitly challenges the nature – though not the fact – of the PT's leadership, in so far as the PT acts like a conventional political party. The Brazilian Workers' Party has thus moved on to ground on which few political leaders have trod.

The PT's ability to respond creatively is shaped by its history. Its containment since its inception of different ideological tendencies on the left has meant that disputes between tendencies have always played a central role in the life of the party. It has a strong belief in democracy, but this can be at the expense of a responsiveness to the new problems and policy arising out of the party's, or rather the government's and the community's, immediate experience. It is a tension between democracy meaning internal norms and rules for defined ideological differences, and democracy meaning an openness to and reflexivity on the innovations and problems of practice.

Participatory budgeting appears to have changed perceptions of the PT itself in Porto Alegre: its popular support has escalated. One measure of this is the continuing choice of a PT mayor in four consecutive elections, with a growing percentage of the vote. Another is the fact that, whereas in 1986 only 6.4 per cent of the Porto Alegre population identified with the PT, research by JB-Vox Populi with significant random samples of the population in August–September 1996 shows 46 per cent making this identification. The growth in PT membership in the city was also impressive: in 1990 the PT in Porto Alegre had 8,817 members; by May 2001 it had 24,033.

At the same time as the party was growing in this phenomenal way, many of the most active, experienced members were becoming part of the local government – there are around 600 politically appointed positions in Porto Alegre's local administration (this is the normal system in local authorities in Brazil). Consequently, when the PT came to office and turned to its own supporters to join the government, about 10 per cent of the local membership moved into government. This creation of a cadre of full-time policy thinkers and doers always runs the risk of creating a two-tier party. It was exacerbated by a tendency battle in which the two tendencies victorious in the competition for the mayoral team – the radical Catholics, supporting mayor Olívio Dutra; and the Maoist-influenced tendency – now mellowed into Gramscians – supporting deputy mayor Tarso Genro. This left the Trotskyist-inclined tendency marginalised in government, even though it is very strong in the party. This process led early in the life of the PT government to what Luciano Brunet, the experienced *petista* who worked for the CRC, described as 'a rupture between party and government, which weakened the party. At times it seemed as if people in government didn't care what the party thought.'

This rift is still felt. There is a growing gulf between government *petistas* and the party outside. Inside, there are intense debates but, says Luciano, 'the ordinary party members can become like spectators'. The weakness of the links between party and government except at election time has been emphasised, Luciano feels, by changes which make the PT like any other traditional social democratic party, with elections for delegates to conference and leading positions only once every three years. Luciano and others believe the PT should be moving in another direction, to become more pluralistic, more closely connected with the NGOs and campaigns that many *petistas* are part of anyway. 'If you want to have a participatory democracy, you need a party which reflects it', concludes Luciano. In his view, if the PT is a conscious brain, it needs to adapt to the fact that in creating a source of democratic power beyond the state, it has dismantled its monopoly of radical brainpower.

The power to deliver

The success of PB in driving Porto Alegre's municipal administration to spend the bulk of its investment budget on making the poor neighbourhoods fit to live in is clear. Most statistics indicate progress significantly ahead of other cities: 9,000 families, who 12 years ago lived in shacks, now have regularised brick housing; nearly the whole population (99 per cent) have treated water; the sewerage system covers 86 per cent of the city, compared with 46 per cent in 1989; the number of school students going on to university doubled between 1989 and 1995; over 50 schools have been built in the past ten years and truancy has fallen from 9 per cent to less than 1 per cent. A detailed analysis of the municipal budget after 1989 shows that the lower the average income of the PB region, the higher the volume of public investment per head. The report concludes that the participatory budget has functioned as 'a powerful instrument of the redistribution of wealth'.

There are also examples of the participatory budget strengthening the hand of the municipality to gain social benefits for the city from private investors. A good example of how PB was used as a launching pad to bargain for social improvements with one of the largest European supermarket chains. In the early 1990s the French company Carrefour wanted to build one of its supermarkets in the north-central region of Porto Alegre. This region has many small businesses, especially shops, and these small entrepreneurs were extremely angry. With the example of PB on their doorstep, they reacted by organising a lively public meeting and decided to take their concerns to the thematic PB plenary of the budget on economic policy. 'We wanted to set up a committee to negotiate for compensation for the small businesses in the area, as a condition of the new supermarket', said one of the activists. 'The participatory budget was the obvious channel for this proposal.'

The outcome was unprecedented. Carrefour had never before had to make real concessions to gain entry into a new marketplace. While normally its supermarkets let spaces inside for around 20 local shops, the Porto Alegre committee won agreement for 40. The company also agreed to employ young people, since they are the ones suffering most from high unemployment, and to help fund training schemes. In the past, the government had successfully bargained for infrastructural improvements from transnationals, such as McDonalds, but it had never before obtained social improvements; it seems likely that the small entrepreneurs gained confidence, moral clout and political backing through discussing their demands and winning the support of the participatory budget.

Conclusions: a new backbone for democracy

In one sense, the civic power which has grown up around the participatory budget depends on the state being willing to share power. There would not be the sustained levels of participation, the popular basis for this civic power, if there were not significant public resources at stake. But the new source of power that develops once this condition is in place has a life and dynamic of its own, which Porto Alegre's local state respects and supports. The rules and meetings of the participatory budget institutionalise its independence and protect it against unilateral action by the state.

The transparency and publicly negotiated character of the rules for PB ensure that it is widely respected and supported. It is perceived to have a legitimacy distinct from the electoral institutions of the mayor and the municipal assembly. The government cannot change PB rules by its own authority – everything has to be negotiated in a process that, until the last legal moment of agreeing the budget, is heavily weighted towards the popular participants. Now, after 12 years of PB, to close the process down would provoke an eruption. And not just in the poor parts of town. PB is an extension of democracy, not a competing structure. It effectively makes the mayor's electoral mandate a daily living pressure on the state apparatus.

Conventionally, elected representatives delegate detailed investment decisions to unelected administrators: PB is in this respect morally more legitimate than representative structures. Added to this moral power is detailed knowledge and know-how, so that municipal councillors and the mayor are no longer dependent only on technical staff but have democratic allies with inside local knowledge who can challenge the administration if it is inefficient or corrupt. This combination of democratic legitimacy and practical knowledge is proving desirable in other areas of the administration too. Participatory decision making has turned out to be a more socially efficient way of running things, delivering a better city to live in.

The democratic legitimacy and valuing of practical knowledge inherent in participatory processes also has the power to strengthen civic power in relation to the private sector. In cases like Carrefour, the participatory process was able to call capitalism's bluff precisely because the legitimacy and longevity of liberal capitalism is rooted in a proclaimed respect for democracy. Big companies rarely claim overtly that, because they have got the money, they can do what they like. The problem is that democracy rarely puts capitalism to the test.

Democracy is more often than not on its knees. In a relatively thriving commercial city like Porto Alegre, it need not be. As a desirable location for investment, it has considerable bargaining power.

It is not easy, nor a quick process, to construct the kind of participatory democracy practised in Porto Alegre. In 1998 the PT won the elections for the government of Rio Grande do Sul, the state that has Porto Alegre as its capital. The new government began to extend PB across the state but faced resistance in many rural areas still dominated by reactionary landowners. It was unable to get the system running as effectively as it had hoped. Although other factors were involved (including bickering between different *petista* factions), the PT lost the state government elections in Rio Grande do Sul in October 2002, as has been mentioned earlier. It was a bitter disappointment for the local *petistas*, tempering their delight at Lula's triumph.

Notes

* This is an edited and shortened version of a chapter of *Reclaim the State: Experiments in People's Democracy*, by Hilary Wainwright, to be published by Verso in May 2003.
1 Margaret Keck, *The Workers' Party and Democratization in Brazil*, Yale University Press, USA, 1991.
2 Since my visit this cycle has been modified so that there is now just one round of public assemblies where the regional delegates and budget councillors are elected and the thematic priorities are chosen. The 'unique round', as it is now called, is preceded by many meetings where the municipal government is called to account for the past year and people begin the debates about priorities and criteria for the election of delegates for the regional fora and the budget council.

Glossary

Aliança de Libertação Nacional (ALN) — National Liberation Alliance

Central Única dos Trabalhadores (CUT) — Workers' Unified Confederation

Comissão Pastoral da Terra (CPT) — Pastoral Land Commission

Comunidade Eclesial de Base (CEB) — Catholic Grassroots Community

Movimento Democrático Brasilero (MDB) — Brazilian Democratic Movement

Movimento dos Trabalhadores Rurais Sem Terra (MST) — Landless Rural Workers' Movement (MST)

Partido Comunista Brasileiro (PCB) — Brazilian Communist Party

Partido Communista Brasilero Revolucionário (PCBR) — Revolutionary Brazilian Communist Party

Partido Comunista do Brasil (PCdoB) — Communist Party of Brazil

Partido do Movimento Democrático Brasileiro (PMDB) — Brazilian Democratic Movement Party

Partido dos Trabalhadores (PT) — Workers' Party

Partido da Social Democracia Brasileiro (PSDB) — Brazilian Social Democracy Party

Partido Socialista Brasileiro (PSB) — Brazilian Socialist Party

Partido Socialista dos Trabalhadores Unificado (PSTU) — Unified Socialist Workers' Party

Bibliography

BRANFORD Sue and Bernardo KUCINSKI, *Carnival of the Oppressed: Lula and the Brazilian Workers' Party,* Latin America Bureau, London, 1995.

BRANFORD, Sue and Jan ROCHA, *Cutting the Wire: the Story of the Landless Movement in Brazil,* Latin America Bureau, London, 2002.

HARNECKER, Marta, *O Sonho era Possível,* MEPLA, Casa América Livre, São Paulo, 1994.

KECK, Margaret,*The Workers' Party and Democratization in Brazil,* Yale University Press, New Haven, 1992.

RESOLUÇÕES DE ENCONTROS E CONGRESSOS (Conference and Congress Resolutions), Partido dos Trabalhadores, Editora Fundação Perseu Abramo, São Paulo, 1998.

SADER, Emir, *Quando novos personagens entram em cena,* Paz e terra, São Paulo, 1988.

SADER, Emir and Ken SILVERSTEIN, *Without Fear of Being Happy: Lula, the Workers' Party and Brazil,* Verso, London and New York, 1991

SHUTT, Harry, *The Trouble with Capitalism: an Enquiry into the Causes of Global Economic Failure,* Zed Books, London and New York, 1998.

SHUTT, Harry, *A New Democracy: Alternatives to a Bankrupt World Order,* Global Issues Series, Zed Books, London and New York, 2001.

SOUZA MARTINS, José de, *O Poder do Atraso: Ensaios de Sociologia da Hist?ria Lenta,* Editora Hucitec, São Paulo, 1999.

WAINWRIGHT, Hilary, *Reclaim the State, Adventures in Popular Democracy,* Verso, London and New York, May 2003.

About the authors

Sue Branford spent ten years in Brazil where she reported for the *Financial Times*, *The Economist* and the *Observer*. After returning to London she worked for the BBC. She has written books on Brazil and Latin America. Her latest book, which she co-authored with Jan Rocha, is *Cutting the Wire: The Story of the Landless Movement in Brazil*.

Bernardo Kucinski lectures in journalism at the School of Communications and Arts at the University of São Paulo. Prior to that, he worked as a journalist for *Veja*, the BBC, *Gazeta Mercantil*, *Exame* and most of the alternative newspapers of the 1970s, some of which he helped to found. He was the *Guardian* correspondent in Brazil for many years. He has written several books, including *A síndrome da Antena parabólica: ética no jornalismo brasileiro*, Editora Fundação Perseu Abramo, São Paulo, 1998.

Hilary Wainwright is the editor of the green left monthly magazine, *Red Pepper*. She is research fellow at the International Labour Studies Centre, Manchester, and Fellow of the Transnational Institute, Amsterdam. She was also a visiting professor at the University of California, Los Angeles. She writes regularly for the *Guardian*. Her books include *Labour: A Tale of Two Parties*; *Beyond the Fragments* (with Sheila Rowbotham and Lynn Segal); *Arguments for a New Left: Answering the Free Market Right*, and several books on radical trade unionism and economic democracy. Her latest book, *Reclaim the State: Experiments in People's Democracy*, is to be published by Verso in June 2003.